More from Magnolia

Recipes from the World-Famous Bakery and Allysa Torey's Home Kitchen

Also by Allysa Torey

The Magnolia Bakery Cookbook (with Jennifer Appel)

More from Magnolia

RECIPES FROM THE WORLD-FAMOUS BAKERY AND ALLYSA TOREY'S HOME KITCHEN

Allysa Torey

SIMON & SCHUSTER
ILLUSTRATED

London · New York · Sydney · Toronto
A CBS COMPANY

SIMON & SCHUSTER
ILLUSTRATED BOOKS
Simon & Schuster UK Ltd
222 Gray's Inn Road
London WC1X 8HB

First published in Great Britain by Simon & Schuster UK Ltd, 2011
A CBS COMPANY

Designed by Jaime Putorti

www.simonandschuster.co.uk

A CIP catalogue record for this book is available from the British Library.

ISBN: 978-0-85720-235-2

Printed in Singapore

For Tadhg,

who says I could never make anything that wasn't good
and whose love helps make my dreams come true

Acknowledgements

I would like to thank my agent, Carla Glasser, and my editor, Sydny Miner, for convincing me to write a second book when I didn't think I wanted to. It turned out to be a very wonderful and creative experience. Special thanks to Barbara DiNicola and my managing staff at Magnolia, whose incredible hard work and support enabled me to take the opportunity to put this project together, and thanks particularly to Margaret Hathaway for her contributions and her assistance and computer skills. Lastly, I would like to thank our loyal customers who have continued to support us over the years despite the crazy long lines out the door.

Contents

Foreword

$\mathcal{A}$ cupcake can change your life. That was an epiphany to which I was not privy in the summer of 1996. Theatre and art are my calling, but in the creative tradition, I needed rent money to sustain those passions. I walked into Magnolia Bakery. I cannot imagine walking out.

On a quiet corner in the residential heart of the West Village in Manhattan, I have played a part in the theatre of sugared success, family dynamic and New York renown. Cherished customers looked wistfully to that first summer when there was no limit on cupcakes per person, when lines never wrapped around the street corner, when the nightly staff was Allysa, my sister Shelly and myself. Visit today, and the cast has quadrupled, the baking is unremitting and as many as five people have the sole task of icing cupcakes. Yet while the number of people who enter the shop has changed drastically, the shop has not. Frequently I am asked about expansion, I just smile. The real thing happens but once.

Magnolia Bakery is tradition. Oh, yes, the business is young, but what is inside is ageless. How beautiful that American tradition thrives in a city known for people who left tradition behind, in a bakery that is alternately Grandma's kitchen and a happening hot spot. It is a place where success has been earned through hard work, where the kitchen is right before your eyes and baking from scratch is priority, and where wealth or fame must wait on line with everybody else.

Because of Magnolia, many of us in the city have a place where every season is joy again. This past holiday a former employee who had left to become a trapeze artist came straight from the airport to Magnolia. How can I not take pride in such a workplace? Although this vision was not my own, I delight at the result of combined efforts. With Allysa's family and my own as colleagues, we have worked through proposals, discoveries, friendships and love gained and lost – all while we are ever mixing, measuring, scooping and icing … forever icing. You can work with your family, and sometimes the people you work with become family, and sometimes becoming passionate about the way you earn your rent can change you. This began as a bit part, and I now find myself in the director's chair, lending what I learn to everything else.

Sometimes when I turn the corner of West 11th Street to another night of sweet chaos, it surprises me, not yet or ever immune. It is the smell of cake baking, I am at work, and I am at home.

Barbara DiNicola
Magnolia General Manager
September 2004

Introduction

When we first opened the Magnolia Bakery, I imagined a cosy, old-fashioned shop where people could come for a cup of coffee and something sweet. I expected our customers to include some local regulars and lots of neighbourhood families. I thought we'd close at seven each evening so I could go home and make dinner. I never expected that Magnolia would turn into a city-wide hangout, much less that on weekend nights there would be lines out the door!

The bakery is busier now than ever. Our customers stop by as much for the feel of the shop as they do for the desserts. With its vintage American decor and desserts, customers often tell me that walking into the bakery is just like stepping back in time to their grandmother's kitchen. They come in for a slice of cake and end up with a little piece of their childhood. Many want to meet me to say thanks for making the red velvet cake they remember from church picnics or the banana pudding just like their mum used to make.

Since the publication of *The Magnolia Bakery Cookbook,* many people have suggested that I do a second book. While working full-time at the bakery, the idea of writing another cookbook seemed impossible. Finally, after putting together a committed staff at the shop, we were able to move full-time to our country house, and I could really consider the idea, knowing that I would have the time and energy necessary to write the book I wanted to write.

The kitchen in my house is the one I've always dreamt of having. It's a big country kitchen with a window over the double white enamel sink that looks out on my vegetable garden and the cornfields beyond. The walls are painted pale yellow, and the glass-fronted cupboards, filled with vintage dishware and linens, are a creamy white. I have a work top just for baking that holds my 1950s Sunbeam Mixmaster, and there is a big enamel table that sits in the middle of the room, which is the perfect place for rolling out pastries.

Being able to work on the book in the country has turned out to be a wonderful experience. It's been great to be able to work on ideas for recipes while sitting on the back porch and then go straight into the kitchen to try them out. I like to create recipes in an old-fashioned style, but with new ideas and perhaps different combinations of ingredients to keep things interesting and fun.

These classic American desserts reflect the sensibilities of the bakery and my home. They aren't fussy or difficult – they're simply my favourites.

Allysa Torey
September 2004

More from
Magnolia

Helpful Hints

Since the first cookbook was published, I've received many, many phone calls from all over the United States and I have frequently been approached at the bakery with questions about specific recipes and baking tips in general. Because of this I've gone over the original Helpful Hints section and tried to go into more depth in areas that might be especially useful to the home baker.

General Baking Hints

At the bakery, even while producing large quantities of desserts, we always use the best and freshest ingredients and we adhere to a set procedure every time.

Before starting it is important to read through the recipe from beginning to end to ensure that you understand it thoroughly. Then assemble all the ingredients (to make sure you have everything!) and the necessary equipment you will need to make the process flow more smoothly.

The butter, eggs and milk should be at room temperature before you even think about beginning a recipe. And if you're making a cheesecake, it is especially important that the cream cheese is at room temperature. Most of the recipes in this book and most cookbooks call for 'softened' butter, but it is important to recognise that softened butter is actually butter at room temperature. If you press your finger into properly softened butter, it will leave an indentation but will retain its shape. If the butter is very soft, it is difficult to achieve the desired texture and density in baked goods. When making icing, let your butter get a bit softer than if you were baking a dessert. If the eggs need to be separated for your recipe, it's easier to separate them when they're cold and then allow them to come to room temperature.

When selecting the tins you will use, keep in mind that metal tins should be smooth, because uneven or blackened tins tend to absorb heat unevenly. I prefer to use glass baking dishes for pies, brownies and squares and I strongly discourage using tins with a non-stick surface. You can grease the tins using a pastry brush or by rubbing in the butter or vegetable fat with your fingers. Just make sure that, either way, the tin's surface is evenly and not overly coated. After greasing, sprinkle a few spoonfuls of flour into the tin, shake it around until the entire inside of the tin is coated with flour and then empty out the excess flour by tapping the tin gently. When called for in the recipe, line the base of the tin with greaseproof paper. If you're making a cake, this is a foolproof way to prevent it sticking to the tin.

Cakes

One of the most important tips that I can offer concerns the creaming of butter. When creaming butter, it is necessary to beat the butter until it is light and fluffy, which takes about three minutes depending on the type of mixer you're using. I have found that most people, especially if they're just learning to bake or if they don't bake very often, don't realise how long three minutes is and so they end up not creaming their butter for the proper amount of time. Creaming the butter properly ensures that the dessert (especially if it's a cake) will have the volume and texture desired. It is also important to add the sugar gradually, to beat continuously and to keep beating for a further two to three minutes. The eggs should then be added, one at a time, beating until the mixture is thick, fluffy and pale in colour. Up to this point it is almost impossible to beat the batter too much.

To make it easier to alternately add the ingredients, I suggest that you thoroughly combine (or sift, if called for) the dry ingredients in a bowl or a large measuring jug and mix the milk, buttermilk or other liquid together with the extract in a separate measuring jug. When adding the wet and dry ingredients, do so alternately, in three parts, beating after each addition. The ingredients should be blended thoroughly and the batter should be smooth, but make sure not to over-beat or the cake will lose its light texture. Remember to use a rubber spatula to scrape down the batter from the sides and the base of the bowl, making sure the ingredients are well blended throughout the mixing process.

When dividing the batter between the prepared tins, you can use a measuring jug if you wish to ensure that you have an equal amount of batter in each tin and your rubber spatula to spread the batter evenly.

It is best to bake cake layers in the centre of the oven, placing the tins on the same rack if possible, but not touching.

Icing

Before icing, make sure that the cake layers are completely cool. Icing will not stick to a warm cake and a warm cake becomes soggy if iced.

Make sure you brush any crumbs off the sides of the cake layers and place the layers top side up (tin side down) on a level surface. If any of the layers are uneven, you can slice off the top using a serrated knife.

I find that the best way to ice a layer cake is by icing between the layers first and then icing the top and sides of the cake. If you make sure to keep plenty of icing on your spatula, the whole icing process will go more smoothly. Keep in mind that this is one of those things that gets easier with practice.

Cookies

First, I highly recommend investing in a small ice cream scoop to use instead of a spoon for measuring your cookies. The one that I use for all of my cookie recipes measures approximately 1 tablespoon in capacity. The ice cream scoop gives you even, rounded cookies that hold their shape well while baking and, obviously, makes all the cookies the same size. (Keep in mind that if you make the cookies much smaller or larger than 1 tablespoon, you must adjust the baking time accordingly.)

Second, if it's summertime and it's really hot and your cookie dough seems too soft, put the dough in the fridge for fifteen to twenty minutes before scooping. If you bake cookies with dough that is too soft, your cookies will spread out too much during baking.

Third, for evenly browned cookies I recommend baking only one tray of cookies at a time on the centre rack of the oven.

Last, the most common problem people seem to have is that they wait too long to take the cookies out of the oven. Pay attention to the recommended baking time. The right time to take cookies out of the oven is when they look almost the way you'd like them to look but still slightly underdone. They may look a little underdone, but cookies continue to bake after they come out of the oven.

Pies

With just a little practice, a golden, flaky pie case is not difficult to achieve. Not having anyone at my house to teach me when I was growing up, it took me a little while to learn how to make pies, too. Although conventional wisdom dictates the use of chilled vegetable fat or butter, I have found that using unchilled vegetable fat results in a dough that is very easy to handle and produces a consistently flaky texture. For my cases I always use butter-flavoured vegetable fat, which gives the butter flavour that I'm looking for but, again, keeps the flakiness that I love.

Most important, I really discourage using a food processor or standing mixer for making pies because it's so easy to overwork the dough when using these methods. Start out with the flour in a bowl, then add the vegetable fat, cut into about one-centimetre (half-inch) pieces. Rub in the vegetable fat until the mixture resembles coarse crumbs (at this point the vegetable fat should be pea-sized). Sprinkle the *ice cold* water, by tablespoons, over the flour mixture, stirring it in gently with a fork. Make sure you do not overwork the dough. Shape the dough into a ball. (If you're making a pie case with a lid, divide the dough into two discs, wrap one in greaseproof paper and set aside.) Place your dough on a lightly floured piece of greaseproof paper, flatten the dough gently with the palm of your hand and sprinkle the top lightly with flour. Using a lightly floured rolling pin, roll out the dough from the centre evenly in all directions. If the dough sticks to the rolling pin, dust it lightly with more flour. Take care to use only as much flour as is necessary to roll out the dough, keeping in mind that adding too much flour during the rolling-out process will produce a dry, tough pastry. Lay your glass pie dish face down on top of the circle of dough, flip the dish over, gently pressing the dough into the dish and then remove the greaseproof paper.

Trim the dough, leaving one centimetre (half an inch) around the edge. If you are making a pie case only, tuck the overhanging pastry dough underneath itself and crimp. If you are making a pie case with a lid, add the filling, mounding it in the centre. Then roll out the second disc, lift the parchment paper with the dough, flip it over the filling and remove the parchment paper. Trim the edges of the dough and pinch together the pastry case and lid.

Cheesecakes

The most frustrating thing about cheesecakes is the tendency for cracks to appear in the cake. The most important thing you can do to avoid these surface cracks is to not over-whip the cream cheese, as this can cause too much air to be incorporated into the batter. Make sure to set the mixer on the lowest speed and to beat the cream cheese until very smooth before adding the other ingredients. Then, when adding the other ingredients, mix only until well incorporated. Extremes in temperature can also lead to surface cracks. Avoid opening the oven door as much as possible while baking and cool the cheesecake gradually in an oven that has been turned off.

The second most frustrating thing is not being quite sure when the cake is actually done. I make them all the time and still stand pondering in front of the oven, jiggling the tin, trying to make sure it's completely cooked yet still perfectly creamy. You can set the timer for an hour, but after that it's really practice and a good judgement call – there's just no fancy advice to give.

Note: If you would like to make individual-sized cheesecakes, as we do at the bakery, divide the cheesecake batter into twelve 7.5 x 7.5-cm (3 x 3-in) cheesecake tins with removable bases and bake for 25 to 30 minutes, or until the edges are set and the centre moves only slightly. The Magic Line individual cheesecake 'pans' that we use are available at www.cooksdream.com and you may find something similar in the UK by doing an internet search.

A few last words . . .

Make sure you check that your oven temperature is correct and if you're not sure, use an oven thermometer. Many ovens are off by a number of degrees, which of course significantly alters your baking time.

Make sure that the oven is preheated to the proper temperature so that your batter is not sitting in the tin or tins at room temperature, waiting to go into the oven. Once the leavening agent is mixed into the batter it is important to get it straight into the oven to start baking.

The time to arrange the oven racks to the right level for whatever you're baking is BEFORE you preheat the oven – not when you're ready to bake your dessert. (Too much heat escapes while you're rearranging the racks if you do it then.)

If it's the first time you're attempting a recipe and you are uncertain of the baking time, test the dessert several times towards the end of the recommended time.

If you do a lot of baking (or cooking) with nuts, like I do, it's a great time saver to toast the nuts in advance so that they're ready anytime you need them for a recipe. Often, if I have the oven on at Gas Mark 4/180°C/fan oven 140°C for something I'm making, I'll take the opportunity to put in a tin of nuts to toast at the same time.

Always use medium eggs for baking. It is important to realise that an egg is a liquid ingredient and substituting large eggs will throw off the balance of a recipe.

Always use unsalted butter, not margarine or vegetable fat (unless vegetable fat is specifically called for in the recipe).

Always use pure vanilla extract, not imitation, which can taste tinny and artificial.

If you would like to make the breakfast buns, like we do them at the bakery, I recommend using a bun tin (which has straight sides) instead of a large muffin tin. Bun tins are available in different sizes.

Coffee Cakes, Quick Breads and Breakfast Buns

Apple Cake with Cinnamon Sugar Topping

I love to get up really early when I have guests visiting for the weekend and make this coffee cake. Using canned sliced apples makes it extremely easy to prepare and it's out of the oven before everyone else wakes up for breakfast.

250 g (9 oz) plain flour
2 teaspoons baking powder
1 teaspoon salt
150 ml (5 fl oz) vegetable oil
    (preferably rapeseed)
200 g (7 oz) sugar
2 eggs, at room temperature

250 ml (9 fl oz) milk
1 teaspoon vanilla extract
565 g (1 lb 4 oz) canned sliced
    apples, drained and patted dry
100 g (3½ oz) sugar mixed with
    1 teaspoon cinnamon

Preheat the oven to Gas Mark 3/160°C/fan oven 140°C.

Grease and lightly flour a 25-cm (10-in) ring mould.

In a small bowl, sift together the flour, baking powder and salt. Set aside.

In a large bowl, using the medium speed of an electric mixer, beat together the oil, sugar and eggs for about 3 minutes until light and thick. Add the dry ingredients in three parts, alternating with the milk and vanilla, beating after each addition until smooth. In a separate small bowl, toss the apples with half of the cinnamon-sugar mixture, then stir half of the apples into the batter. Pour the batter into the prepared tin. Drop the remaining apples on top of the batter and sprinkle with the remaining cinnamon sugar. Bake for 60–70 minutes, or until a skewer inserted in the centre of the cake comes out clean. Let the cake cool in the tin for 1 hour, then remove from the tin and cool completely on a wire rack.

MAKES ONE 25-CM (10-IN) CAKE

Banana Bread
with Coconut and Pecans

Honestly, I was never a big banana bread fan until the idea of adding coconut came to me one afternoon and inspired this recipe, which turned out wonderfully. It's surprisingly good with a little salted butter as well as plain.

375 g (13 oz) flour
1 ½ teaspoons bicarbonate of soda
¾ teaspoon cinnamon
¾ teaspoon salt
175 ml (6 fl oz) rapeseed oil
300 g (10½ oz) sugar
3 eggs, at room temperature, well
    beaten

1 ½ teaspoons vanilla extract
375 g (13 oz) mashed ripe bananas
175 ml (6 fl oz) sour cream
175 g (6 oz) toasted pecan nuts,
    coarsely chopped (see Note)
65 g (2¼ oz) desiccated coconut

Note: To toast the pecan nuts, place on a baking tray in an oven at Gas Mark 4/180°C/fan oven 160°C for 15 minutes, or until lightly browned and fragrant.

Preheat the oven to Gas Mark 4/180°C/fan oven 160°C.

Grease and lightly flour a 25-cm (10-in) ring mould.

In a medium-sized bowl, sift together the flour, bicarbonate of soda, cinnamon and salt. Set aside.

In a large bowl, using the medium speed of an electric mixer, beat together the oil and sugar. Add the eggs and vanilla and beat well. Add the bananas and sour cream and mix well. Add the dry ingredients and mix until just combined. Stir in the pecans and coconut. Pour the batter into the prepared tin. Bake for 60–70 minutes, or until a skewer inserted into the centre of the bread comes out with moist crumbs attached. Leave to cool for at least 1 hour before removing from the tin and serving.

MAKES ONE 25-CM (10-IN) CAKE

Pear Streusel Breakfast Buns

$\mathcal{A}$ really nice, not-too-sweet breakfast treat. You can substitute apples for the pears if you like.

STREUSEL TOPPING
225 g (8 oz) light brown sugar
1 1/2 teaspoons cinnamon
55 g (2 oz) unsalted butter, softened and cut into small pieces
185 g (6 1/2 oz) walnuts, chopped

BUNS
185 g (6 1/2 oz) plain flour

1/4 teaspoon bicarbonate of soda
1/4 teaspoon salt
175 g (6 oz) unsalted butter, softened
200 g (7 oz) sugar
3 eggs, at room temperature
6 tablespoons milk
1 teaspoon vanilla extract
250 g (9 oz) peeled pears, coarsely chopped

Preheat the oven to Gas Mark 4/180°C/fan oven 160°C.

Grease and lightly flour 12 bun tins or large muffin tins.

To make the topping, in a medium-sized bowl, combine the brown sugar and cinnamon. Rub in the butter until the mixture resembles coarse crumbs. Add the walnuts and, using your hands, toss until the ingredients are well combined. Set aside.

To make the buns, in a small bowl, combine the flour, bicarbonate of soda and salt. Set aside.

In a large bowl, using the medium speed of an electric mixer, cream the butter until smooth. Add the sugar gradually and beat for about 3 minutes until fluffy. Add the eggs, one at a time, beating well after each addition.

Add the dry ingredients in two parts, alternating with the milk and vanilla, beating until well incorporated. Stir in the pears. Spoon the batter into the bun tins or muffin tins. Sprinkle the topping over the buns, making sure to keep the crumbs within the muffin tins (otherwise the buns are difficult to remove from the tins).

Bake for 20–25 minutes, or until a skewer inserted in the centre of a bun comes out clean.

MAKES 12 BUNS

Courgette Walnut Bread

This is a recipe that I've been making since I was a teenager and I've tweaked it here and there over the years. If you have a vegetable garden and can pick your own fresh courgettes, it makes all the difference.

125 g (4½ oz) plain flour
1 teaspoon bicarbonate of soda
½ teaspoon baking powder
½ teaspoon salt
½ teaspoon cinnamon
125 ml (4 fl oz) vegetable oil
   (preferably rapeseed)

150 g (5 oz) sugar
2 eggs, at room temperature
½ teaspoon vanilla extract
125 g (4½ oz) shredded courgette
   (including skin)
100 g (3½ oz) walnuts, chopped

Preheat the oven to Gas Mark 4/180°C/fan oven 160°C.

Grease and flour a 900-g (2-lb) loaf tin.

In a small bowl, combine the flour, bicarbonate of soda, baking powder, salt and cinnamon. Set aside.

In a large bowl, using the medium speed of an electric mixer, beat together the oil, sugar, eggs and vanilla for about 3 minutes until light and thick. Stir in the courgette.

Add the dry ingredients and mix until just combined. Stir in the walnuts.

Pour the batter into the prepared tin. Place on a baking tray and bake for 50–60 minutes, or until a skewer inserted in the centre of the loaf comes out with moist crumbs attached. Leave to cool for at least 1 hour before serving.

MAKES 1 LOAF

Blueberry Coffee Cake
with Vanilla Glaze

This light and moist coffee cake is simple to prepare and makes a good addition to breakfast or brunch.

CAKE

250 g (9 oz) plain flour
2 teaspoons baking powder
1 teaspoon salt
150 ml (5 fl oz) vegetable oil
    (preferably rapeseed)
200 g (7 oz) sugar
2 eggs, at room temperature
250 ml (9 fl oz) milk

1 teaspoon vanilla extract
225 g (8 oz) fresh blueberries, lightly
    coated with flour

VANILLA GLAZE

160 g (5½ oz) icing sugar, sifted
125 ml (4 fl oz) double cream
½ teaspoon vanilla extract

Preheat the oven to Gas Mark 3/160°C/fan oven 140°C.

Grease and lightly flour a 25-cm (10-in) ring mould.

In a small bowl, sift together the flour, baking powder and salt. Set aside.

In a large bowl, using the medium speed of an electric mixer, beat together the oil, sugar and eggs for about 3 minutes until light and thick. Add the dry ingredients in three parts, alternating with the milk and vanilla, beating after each addition until smooth. Fold in the blueberries. Pour the batter into the prepared tin and bake for 60–70 minutes or until a skewer inserted in the centre of the cake comes out clean. Let the cake cool in the tin for 1 hour. Remove from the tin and cool completely on a wire rack.

To make the vanilla glaze, in the top of a double boiler, over barely simmering water, combine the sugar, cream and vanilla. Stir for about 2 minutes until the ingredients are well blended. Pour into a glass measuring jug and cover until ready to use. When the cake is completely cool, drizzle the glaze decoratively over the cake. Allow the glaze to set for 1 hour before slicing and serving the cake.

MAKES ONE 25-CM (10-IN) CAKE

Cream Cheese Crumb Buns

This recipe was inspired, believe it or not, by a ready-prepared crumb cheese coffee cake. A few years back, some of the staff were at my house (when I first moved and didn't yet have a kitchen) and we were eating the ready-prepared cake (right out of the packet, of course) and said, 'This is really good. We could make this at the bakery.' So we came up with this recipe.

CREAM CHEESE FILLING
225 g (8 oz) cream cheese, softened
40 g (1½ oz) unsalted butter, softened
2 tablespoons sugar
1 egg yolk, at room temperature
½ teaspoon vanilla extract

CRUMB TOPPING
185 g (6½ oz) plain flour
225 g (8 oz) soft light brown sugar
2 teaspoons baking powder
115 g (4 oz) unsalted butter, softened and cut into small pieces

BUNS
185 g (6½ oz) plain flour
1 teaspoon baking powder
¼ teaspoon salt
125 ml (4 fl oz) vegetable fat
100 g (3½ oz) sugar
2 eggs, at room temperature
125 ml (4 fl oz) milk

Preheat the oven to Gas Mark 4/180°C/fan oven 160°C.

Grease and lightly flour 16 bun tins or large muffin tins.

To make the filling, in a medium-sized bowl, beat the cream cheese and butter until smooth and creamy. Add the sugar, egg yolk and vanilla and beat well. Set aside.

To make the topping, in a large bowl, mix together the flour, sugar and baking powder. Rub in the butter until the mixture resembles coarse crumbs. Set aside.

To make the buns, in a small bowl, combine the flour, baking powder and salt. Set aside.

In a large bowl, using the medium speed of an electric mixer, beat together the vegetable fat and sugar until smooth. Add the eggs, one at a time, beating well after each addition. Add the dry ingredients, in two parts, alternating with the milk and beating until well incorporated. Spoon the batter into the bun tins or muffin tins. Bake for 10 minutes.

Remove from the oven and working quickly but carefully, place a tablespoon of the cream cheese filling in the centre of each bun and press it down gently with the back of the spoon. Sprinkle the crumb topping over the cream cheese, covering the entire top of the bun and making sure to keep the crumbs within the muffin tins (otherwise the buns are difficult to remove from the tins). Return to the oven and bake for a further 13 minutes. (Do not use a skewer to check for doneness – it will only come out with cream cheese filling attached!)

Allow to cool for 30 minutes before serving. These are best when eaten warm with the filling still a little gooey.

MAKES 16 BUNS

Brown Sugar
Pecan Cake

I love cake that is not too sweet or too fancy and can be eaten at the kitchen table in the afternoon with tea or coffee. This can also be served with whipped cream if you wish.

275 g (9 ½ oz) superfine plain flour
2 teaspoons baking powder
½ teaspoon salt
175 g (6 oz) unsalted butter, softened
325 g (11 ½ oz) soft light brown sugar
2 eggs, at room temperature

250 ml (9 fl oz) milk
1 teaspoon vanilla extract
175 g (6 oz) toasted pecan nuts, chopped (see Note)

Note: To toast the pecan nuts, place on a baking tray in an oven at Gas Mark 4/180°C/fan oven 160°C for 15 minutes, or until lightly browned and fragrant.

Preheat the oven to Gas Mark 3/160°C/fan oven 140°C.

Grease and lightly flour a 25-cm (10-in) ring mould.

In a small bowl, sift together the flour, baking powder and salt. Set aside.

In a large bowl, using the medium speed of an electric mixer, cream the butter until smooth. Add the sugar gradually and beat for about 3 minutes until fluffy. Add the eggs, one at a time, beating well after each addition. Add the dry ingredients in three parts, alternating with the milk and vanilla, beating after each addition until smooth. Reserving 4 tablespoons of the pecans, stir in the remaining pecans. Pour the batter into the prepared tin and sprinkle the reserved pecans over the top.

Bake for 60–70 minutes, or until a skewer inserted in the centre of the cake comes out clean. Let the cake cool in the tin for 1 hour. Remove from the tin and cool completely on a wire rack.

MAKES ONE 25-CM (10-IN) CAKE

Raspberry Cream Cheese Breakfast Buns

These buns have been our most popular breakfast item at the bakery since the first day we opened our doors. The flavours of the cream cheese and the preserves work really well together.

Bun

225 g (8 oz) plain flour
1 teaspoon baking powder
½ teaspoon bicarbonate of soda
¼ teaspoon salt
225 g (8 oz) cream cheese, softened
115 g (4 oz) unsalted butter, softened
200 g (7 oz) sugar
2 eggs, at room temperature

4 tablespoons milk
½ teaspoon vanilla extract

Topping

160 g (5½ oz) raspberry preserves

Decoration

Icing sugar

Preheat the oven to Gas Mark 4/180°C/fan oven 160°C.

Grease and lightly flour 9 bun tins or large muffin tins.

In a small bowl, combine the flour, baking powder, bicarbonate of soda and salt. Set aside.

In a large bowl, using the medium speed of an electric mixer, beat together the cream cheese, butter and sugar for about 3 minutes until smooth. Add the eggs and beat well. Add the dry ingredients in two parts, alternating with the milk and vanilla. Spoon the batter into the bun tins or muffin tins, filling them about two-thirds full. Drop 3 small dollops (about a teaspoonful each) of raspberry preserves on to the top of each bun and, using the tip of a sharp knife, swirl the preserves into the batter, forming a decorative pattern. Bake for 25–30 minutes or until a skewer inserted in the centre of the bun comes out clean.

Allow the buns to cool for about 30 minutes before sprinkling with icing sugar and serving.

Makes 9 buns

Cookies

Chocolate Chocolate Chip Drop Cookies

An old-fashioned, chewy chocolate cookie with little extra bursts of chocolate from the miniature chips.

125 g (4½ oz) plain flour
40 g (1½ oz) cocoa powder
½ teaspoon baking powder
¼ teaspoon salt
75 g (2½ oz) unsalted butter, softened
65 g (2¼ oz) vegetable fat

200 g (7 oz) sugar plus 1 tablespoon (for sprinkling)
1 egg, at room temperature
1 teaspoon vanilla extract
85 g (3 oz) miniature plain chocolate chips

In a small bowl, combine the flour, cocoa, baking powder and salt. Set aside.

In a large bowl, cream the butter, vegetable fat and sugar for about 3 minutes until smooth. Add the egg and vanilla and beat well. Add the dry ingredients and mix thoroughly. Stir in the chocolate chips. Drop by rounded teaspoonfuls on to ungreased baking trays, leaving several centimetres between for expansion. Sprinkle lightly with the sugar. Place the baking trays in the refrigerator and chill for 20 minutes.

Preheat the oven to Gas Mark 4/180°C/fan oven 160°C.

Bake for 10–12 minutes. Cool the cookies on the trays for 5 minutes and then remove to a wire rack to cool completely.

MAKES 24 COOKIES

Iced Ginger Cookies

I've been making these cookies for years now and I still get really excited every autumn when I bake the first batch of the season. They're chewy and spicy with just the right amount of sweet icing. (My boyfriend, Tadhg, insists that I mention he prefers them without the icing.)

COOKIE

250 g (9 oz) plain flour
2 teaspoons bicarbonate of soda
1 teaspoon ground ginger
1 teaspoon cinnamon
$^1/_2$ teaspoon salt
175 ml (6 fl oz) vegetable oil
   (preferably rapeseed)

200 g (7 oz) sugar plus 1 tablespoon
   (for sprinkling)
1 egg, at room temperature
125 ml (4 fl oz) molasses

ICING

65 g (2$^1/_4$ oz) icing sugar, sifted
1 tablespoon vegetable fat
2 teaspoons water

Preheat the oven to Gas Mark 4/180°C/fan oven 160°C.

In a small bowl, combine the flour, bicarbonate of soda, ginger, cinnamon and salt. Set aside.

In a large bowl, using the medium speed of an electric mixer, beat together the oil and sugar for 2–3 minutes. Add the egg and molassese and beat well. Add the dry ingredients and mix thoroughly. Drop by rounded teaspoonfuls on to ungreased baking trays, leaving several centimetres between for expansion. Sprinkle lightly with sugar. Bake for 12 minutes. Cool the cookies on the sheets for 5 minutes and then remove to a wire rack to cool completely.

To make the icing, combine the sugar, vegetable fat and water and beat until smooth and creamy. Cover until ready to use.

When the cookies are completely cool, spread a very thin layer of icing on each cookie with a small knife or spatula. Allow the icing to set before stacking the cookies or they will stick together.

MAKES 30 COOKIES

Coconut Oatmeal Drop Cookies

I'm always striving to make the perfect crispy but chewy oatmeal cookie. I'm not fond of raisins, so I add coconut instead for extra texture and sweetness.

185 g (6½ oz) plain flour
1 teaspoon bicarbonate of soda
1 teaspoon cinnamon
¼ teaspoon salt
225 g (8 oz) unsalted butter, softened
225 g (8 oz) light brown sugar
100 g (3½ oz) granulated sugar

1 egg, at room temperature
1½ teaspoons vanilla extract
125 g (4½ oz) porridge oats
100 g (3½ oz) desiccated coconut

Preheat the oven to Gas Mark 5/190°C/fan oven 170°C.

In a small bowl, combine the flour, bicarbonate of soda, cinnamon and salt. Set aside.

In a large bowl, cream the butter with the sugars for about 2 minutes until smooth. Add the egg and vanilla and beat well. Add the dry ingredients and mix thoroughly. Stir in the oats and coconut. Drop by rounded teaspoonfuls on to ungreased baking trays, leaving several centimetres between for expansion. Bake for 12–14 minutes or until lightly golden.

Cool the cookies on the baking trays for 5 minutes and then remove to a wire rack to cool completely.

MAKES 42 COOKIES

Snickerdoodles

*T*his soft cinnamon-sugar cookie has been around for ages and I don't think anyone knows where the name comes from. When I was growing up, we always made these at Christmastime, so we still do that at the bakery.

310 g (11 oz) plain flour
2 teaspoons cream of tartar
1 teaspoon bicarbonate of soda
¼ teaspoon salt
225 g (8 oz) unsalted butter, softened
300 g (10½ oz) sugar
2 eggs, at room temperature

2 tablespoons milk
1 teaspoon vanilla extract

75 g (2½ oz) sugar mixed with
    2 teaspoons cinnamon, for
    sprinkling

In a small bowl, combine the flour, cream of tartar, bicarbonate of soda and salt. Set aside.

In a large bowl, cream the butter and sugar for about 2 minutes until smooth. Add the eggs, milk and vanilla and beat well. Add the dry ingredients and mix thoroughly. Wrap the dough tightly with cling film and chill in the refrigerator for 2 hours.

Preheat the oven to Gas Mark 4/180°C/fan oven 160°C.

Drop by rounded teaspoonfuls on to ungreased baking trays, leaving several centimetres between for expansion. (I recommend leaving extra room between these cookies because they spread more than most.) Sprinkle generously with the cinnamon-sugar mixture. Bake for 12–14 minutes.

Cool the cookies on the baking trays for 5 minutes and then remove to a wire rack to cool completely.

MAKES 36 COOKIES

White Chocolate Pecan Drop Cookies

Two of my favourite ingredients – toasted pecan nuts and creamy white chocolate – together in what is definitely the most often baked cookie at our house.

185 g (6½ oz) plain flour
1 teaspoon bicarbonate of soda
½ teaspoon salt
150 g (5 oz) unsalted butter, softened
100 g (3½ oz) granulated sugar
115 g (4 oz) soft light brown sugar
1 egg, at room temperature

1 teaspoon vanilla extract
115 g (4 oz) toasted pecan nuts, coarsely chopped (see Note)
115 g (4 oz) white chocolate (preferably Lindt), coarsely chopped

Note: To toast the pecan nuts, place them on a baking tray in an oven at Gas Mark 4/180°C/ fan oven 160°C for 15 minutes, or until lightly browned and fragrant.

Preheat the oven to Gas Mark 4/180°C/fan oven 160°C.

In a small bowl, combine the flour, bicarbonate of soda and salt. Set aside.

In a large bowl, cream the butter with the sugars for about two minutes until smooth. Add the egg and vanilla and beat well. Add the dry ingredients and mix thoroughly. Stir in the pecans and white chocolate. Drop by rounded teaspoonfuls on to ungreased baking trays, leaving several centimetres between for expansion. Bake for 10–12 minutes or until lightly golden.

Cool the cookies on the baking trays for 5 minutes and then remove to a wire rack to cool completely.

MAKES 36 COOKIES

Raspberry Hazelnut Linzer Cookies

Another big Christmastime favourite at the bakery, these cookies require a few steps but are really not difficult to make and are quite festive.

375 g (13 oz) plain flour
¼ teaspoon salt
350 g (12 oz) unsalted butter, softened
200 g (7 oz) granulated sugar
1 ½ teaspoons vanilla extract

115 g (4 oz) toasted hazelnuts, finely chopped (see Note)
100 g (3 ½ oz) raspberry preserves
65 g (2 ¼ oz) icing sugar (for dusting)

Note: To toast the hazelnuts, place them on a baking tray in an oven at Gas Mark 4/180°C/ fan oven 160°C for 15 minutes or until lightly browned and fragrant.

In a small bowl, combine the flour and salt. Set aside.

In a large bowl, cream the butter and sugar for about 2 minutes until smooth. Add the vanilla and beat well. Add the dry ingredients in three parts, adding the nuts with the last portion, and mix until just combined. Shape the dough into two flat discs, wrap each disc tightly in cling film and refrigerate for 30 minutes.

Working with one disc at a time, roll out the dough on a lightly floured surface to 5-mm (¼-in) thickness. Using a 7.5-cm (3-in) fluted cutter, cut out the cookies and place them on baking trays lined with greaseproof paper. Place the baking trays in the refrigerator and chill for a further 15 minutes.

Preheat the oven to Gas Mark 4/180°C/fan oven 160°C.

Remove the baking trays from the refrigerator and using a 1-cm (½-in) fluted cutter, cut a circle out of the centre of half of the cookies. Arrange on ungreased baking trays, 5 cm (2 in) apart and bake for 15–18 minutes or until lightly golden around the edges.

Cool the cookies on the baking trays for 5 minutes and then remove to a wire rack to cool completely.

Spread 1 teaspoon of preserves on the flat side of the cookies without the cut-out centres. Sandwich the cut-out cookies with the cookies spread with the preserves. Dust the cookies on both sides with the icing sugar.

MAKES 20 COOKIES

Toffee Pecan Drop Cookies

*I*f you can't find the toffee pieces in your supermarket's baking section, you can substitute chopped chocolate-coated toffees – but I love these cookies without any chocolate in them.

250 g (9 oz) plain flour
1 teaspoon bicarbonate of soda
½ teaspoon salt
225 g (8 oz) butter
175 g (6 oz) soft light brown sugar
50 g (1 ¾ oz) granulated sugar

1 egg, at room temperature
1 ½ teaspoons vanilla extract
175 g (6 oz) toasted pecan nuts,
    coarsely chopped (see Note)
160 g (5 ½ oz) toffee pieces

Note: To toast the pecan nuts, place them on a baking tray in an oven at Gas Mark 4/180°C/ fan oven 160°C for 15 minutes or until lightly browned and fragrant.

Preheat the oven to Gas Mark 4/180°C/fan oven 160°C.

In a small bowl, combine the flour, bicarbonate of soda and salt. Set aside.

In a large bowl, cream the butter with the sugars for about 2 minutes until smooth. Add the egg and vanilla and beat well. Add the dry ingredients and mix thoroughly. Stir in the pecans and toffee. Drop by rounded teaspoonfuls on to ungreased baking trays, leaving several centimetres between for expansion. Bake for 10–12 minutes or until lightly golden.

Cool the cookies on the baking trays for 5 minutes and then remove to a wire rack to cool completely.

Makes 48 cookies

Oatmeal Peanut Butter Chip Cookies

After countless evenings of standing in front of the open refrigerator, dipping freshly baked oatmeal cookies into the jar of peanut butter . . .

125 g (4 1/2 oz) plain flour
1/2 teaspoon bicarbonate of soda
1/2 teaspoon salt
1/4 teaspoon cinnamon
175 g (6 oz) unsalted butter, softened
160 g (5 1/2 oz) soft light brown sugar
100 g (3 1/2 oz) granulated sugar

1 egg, at room temperature
1 1/2 teaspoons vanilla extract
215 g (7 1/2 oz) quick-cooking porridge oats
175 g (6 oz) peanut butter chips or white chocolate chips

Preheat the oven to Gas Mark 4/180°C/fan oven 160°C.

In a small bowl, combine the flour, bicarbonate of soda, salt and cinnamon. Set aside.

In a large bowl, cream the butter with the sugars for about 2 minutes until smooth. Add the egg and vanilla and beat well. Add the dry ingredients and mix thoroughly. Stir in the oats and peanut butter chips. Drop by rounded teaspoonfuls on to ungreased baking trays, leaving several centimetres between for expansion. Bake for 11–13 minutes.

Cool the cookies on the baking trays for 5 minutes and then remove to a wire rack to cool completely.

MAKES 36 COOKIES

Pumpkin Walnut Cookies with Brown Butter Icing

*T*his spicy, cake-like cookie comes from Nancy Sinko, the mother of Barbara and Shelly, who have worked with me at the bakery since the very beginning. Nancy ices these cookies with a cream cheese icing – either way, they're really good.

COOKIE
310 g (11 oz) plain flour
1 tablespoon baking powder
1 teaspoon salt
1 teaspoon mixed spice
½ teaspoon cinnamon
¼ teaspoon ground ginger
55 g (2 oz) unsalted butter, softened
325 g (11 ½ oz) soft light brown sugar
2 eggs, at room temperature
225 g (8 oz) canned pumpkin purée
2 teaspoons vanilla extract
125 g (4 ½ oz) walnuts, chopped

ICING
250 g (9 oz) icing sugar
3 tablespoons milk
1 teaspoon vanilla extract
40 g (1 ½ oz) unsalted butter

DECORATION
Walnut halves

Preheat the oven to Gas Mark 5/190°C/fan oven 170°C.

To make the cookies, in a small bowl, combine the flour, baking powder, salt, mixed spice, cinnamon and ginger. Set aside.

In a large bowl, cream the butter and sugar until evenly combined. Add the eggs, pumpkin and vanilla and beat well. Add the dry ingredients and mix thoroughly. Stir in the walnuts. Drop by rounded teaspoonfuls on to ungreased baking trays, leaving several centimetres between for expansion. The batter will seem extremely soft compared with most cookie doughs, but it will firm up during baking. Bake for 12 minutes. Cool the cookies on the baking trays for 10–12 minutes and then remove to a wire rack to cool completely.

To make the icing, place the sugar, milk and vanilla in a small bowl. Set aside. In a small saucepan over a medium-high heat, cook the butter for about 3–5 minutes until lightly browned. Remove from the heat, add to the other ingredients and beat until smooth and creamy. Cover until ready to use.

When the cookies are completely cool, spread a generous amount of icing on each cookie and top with a walnut half. Let the icing set before stacking the cookies or they will stick together.

MAKES 48 COOKIES

Peanut Butter Chocolate Chip Pecan Cookies

For those of you who, like me, can't resist adding peanut butter to desserts, this is basically a chocolate chip cookie with peanut butter chips as well. Also, the milk in the batter gives these cookies a lovely texture.

310 g (11 oz) plain flour
1 teaspoon bicarbonate of soda
1/2 teaspoon salt
225 g (8 oz) unsalted butter, softened
225 g (8 oz) soft light brown sugar
65 g (2 1/4 oz) granulated sugar
1 egg, at room temperature

2 tablespoons milk
1 1/2 teaspoons vanilla extract
175 g (6 oz) toasted pecan nuts,
    coarsely chopped (see Note)
175 g (6 oz) peanut butter chips or
    white chocolate chips
65 g (2 1/4 oz) plain chocolate chips

Note: To toast the pecan nuts, place them on a baking tray in an oven at Gas Mark 4/180°C/ fan oven 160°C for 15 minutes or until lightly browned and fragrant.

Preheat the oven to Gas Mark 4/180°C/fan oven 160°C.

In a small bowl, combine the flour, bicarbonate of soda and salt. Set aside.

In a large bowl, cream the butter with the sugars for about 2 minutes until smooth. Add the egg, milk and vanilla and beat well. Add the dry ingredients and mix thoroughly. Stir in the pecans, peanut butter chips and chocolate chips. Drop by rounded teaspoonfuls on to ungreased baking trays, leaving several centimetres between for expansion. Bake for 10–12 minutes, or until lightly golden.

Cool the cookies on the baking trays for 5 minutes and then remove to a wire rack to cool completely.

MAKES 60 COOKIES

Brownies
and
Bars

White Chocolate Pecan Bars

This cookie bar has a really nice brown sugar shortbread base with a topping of white chocolate and pecan nuts.

BAR

250 g (9 oz) plain flour
½ teaspoon salt
225 g (8 oz) unsalted butter, softened
225 g (8 oz) light brown sugar
1 egg, at room temperature
1 teaspoon vanilla extract

65 g (2¼ oz) toasted pecan nuts, coarsely chopped (see Note)

TOPPING

275 g (9½ oz) white chocolate, coarsely chopped
65 g (2¼ oz) toasted pecan nuts, coarsely chopped (see Note)

Note: To toast the pecan nuts, place them on a baking tray in an oven at Gas Mark 4/180°C/fan oven 160°C for 15 minutes or until lightly browned and fragrant.

Preheat the oven to Gas Mark 4/180°C/fan oven 160°C.

Grease and lightly flour a 33 x 23-cm (13 x 9-in) baking tin.

In a small bowl, combine the flour and salt. Set aside.

In a large bowl, beat together the butter, sugar, egg and vanilla for 2–3 minutes until creamy. Add the dry ingredients and mix thoroughly. Stir in the pecans. Spread the batter evenly in the prepared tin. Bake for 25 minutes.

Remove from the oven and immediately sprinkle the white chocolate on top. Allow to stand for 5 minutes and then gently spread the melted chocolate in a thin layer over the bars. Sprinkle with the pecans.

Allow to cool to room temperature (the white chocolate should harden) or overnight before cutting and serving.

MAKES TWENTY-FOUR 5-CM (2-IN) BARS

Apple Bars with Oatmeal Crumb Topping

A perfect autumn treat – all the flavours of apple pie, but unlike the more fragile pie, these bars are easily wrapped up for lunches and picnics.

BASE
225 g (8 oz) unsalted butter, softened and cut into small pieces
250 g (9 oz) plain flour

TOPPING
185 g (6½ oz) plain flour
225 g (8 oz) soft light brown sugar
30 g (1¼ oz) porridge oats plus
    3 tablespoons (for sprinkling)
½ teaspoon cinnamon

150 g (5 oz) unsalted butter, softened and cut into small pieces

FILLING
600 g (1 lb 5 oz) canned apple pie filling

GLAZE
125 g (4½ oz) icing sugar, sifted
1 tablespoon plus 1 teaspoon water

Preheat the oven to Gas Mark 4/180°C/fan oven 160°C.

To make the base, in a large bowl, using the medium speed of an electric mixer, beat together the butter and flour until crumbly and well combined. Transfer the mixture to an ungreased 33 x 23-cm (13 x 9-in) baking tin and, using your hands, pat the base firmly and evenly into the tin.

Bake the base for 20 minutes. Remove from the oven and allow to stand for about 45 minutes to cool completely.

To make the topping, in a large bowl, mix together the flour, sugar, oats and cinnamon. Rub in the butter until the mixture resembles coarse crumbs, then toss until all the ingredients are well combined. Set aside.

When the base is cool, gently and evenly spread the apple filling over it, leaving a 5-mm (¼-in) edge all around. Sprinkle the crumb topping over the filling, then sprinkle the additional 3 tablespoons of oats over the crumb topping. Bake for 45 minutes. Allow to cool to room temperature.

To make the glaze, combine the sugar and water and beat until smooth. Cover until ready to use. When the bars are completely cool, drizzle the glaze decoratively over the crumb topping. Allow the glaze to set for 15–20 minutes before cutting and serving.

MAKES TWENTY-FOUR 5-CM (2-IN) BARS

Blondies with Cream Cheese Swirl and Pecans

There have been lots of recipes over the years for cream cheese swirl brownies, but never the blondie and cream cheese combination, which seemed perfect to me. If, like me, you are not a huge chocolate fan, you'll love these.

CREAM CHEESE FILLING
115 g (4 oz) cream cheese (not softened)
2 tablespoons sugar
1 egg yolk, at room temperature
1 tablespoon plain flour

BLONDIES
200 g (7 oz) superfine plain flour
1 teaspoon baking powder

$\frac{1}{4}$ teaspoon salt
175 g (6 oz) unsalted butter, softened
275 g (9½ oz) soft light brown sugar
50 g (1¾ oz) granulated sugar
2 eggs, at room temperature
2 teaspoons vanilla extract
65 g (2¼ oz) toasted pecan nuts, coarsely chopped (see Note)

Note: To toast the pecan nuts, place them on a baking tray in an oven at Gas Mark 4/180°C/ fan oven 160°C for 15 minutes, or until lightly browned and fragrant.

Preheat the oven to Gas Mark 4/180°C/fan oven 160°C.

Grease and lightly flour a 33 x 23-cm (13 x 9-in) baking tin.

To make the cream cheese filling, in a medium-sized bowl, beat the cream cheese and sugar until smooth. Add the egg yolk and flour and beat well. Set aside.

To make the blondies, in a small bowl, combine the flour, baking powder and salt. Set aside. In a large bowl, cream the butter with the sugars for about 2 minutes until smooth. Add the eggs and vanilla and beat well. Add the dry ingredients and mix thoroughly. Spread the batter evenly in the prepared tin.

Drop the cream cheese mixture by teaspoonfuls over the batter. Using a small knife, swirl the cream cheese into the batter, forming a decorative pattern. Sprinkle the pecans evenly over the batter.

Bake for 35–40 minutes or until a skewer inserted in the centre of the tin comes out with moist crumbs attached. Do not over-bake. Allow to cool to room temperature or overnight before cutting and serving.

MAKES TWENTY-FOUR 5-CM (2-IN) BLONDIES

Walnut Brown Sugar Squares

This is, hands down, the quickest and easiest recipe in this book. You don't even need to wait for the butter to soften because there's no butter (or any vegetable fat) in it!

75 g (2¾ oz) plain flour
¼ teaspoon bicarbonate of soda
¼ teaspoon salt
225 g (8 oz) soft light brown sugar

1 egg, at room temperature
1 teaspoon vanilla extract
125 g (4½ oz) walnuts, chopped

Preheat the oven to Gas Mark 4/180°C/fan oven 160°C.

Lightly grease a 20 x 20-cm (8 x 8-in) baking tin.

In a small bowl, combine the flour, bicarbonate of soda and salt. Set aside.

In a medium-sized bowl, using the medium speed of an electric mixer, beat together the sugar, egg and vanilla for about 2 minutes until creamy and smooth. Add the dry ingredients and mix thoroughly. Reserve 2 tablespoons of the walnuts and stir in the remainder. Transfer the batter to the prepared tin and, using your hands, spread the batter evenly. Sprinkle with the remaining 2 tablespoons of walnuts. Bake for 25 minutes. The centre will not be set but do not over-bake.

Allow to cool to room temperature, cover tightly with cling film and leave to set overnight before cutting and serving.

MAKES SIXTEEN 5-CM (2-IN) SQUARES

Chocolate Fudge Brownies with Butterscotch Chips and Pecans

These are really dense, really fudgy brownies. I've always loved the combination of butterscotch and chocolate.

65 g (2¼ oz) plain flour
⅛ teaspoon salt
55 g (2 oz) unsalted butter
285 g (10 oz) plain chocolate
2 eggs, at room temperature
200 g (7 oz) sugar

2 teaspoons vanilla extract
115 g (4 oz) toasted pecan nuts,
    coarsely chopped (see Note)
30 g (1¼ oz) butterscotch chips or
    white chocolate chips

Note: To toast the pecan nuts, place them on a baking tray in an oven at Gas Mark 4/180°C/ fan oven 160°C for 15 minutes, or until lightly browned and fragrant.

Preheat the oven to Gas Mark 3/160°C/fan oven 140°C.

Grease and lightly flour a 20 x 20-cm (8 x 8-in) baking tin.

In a small bowl, combine the flour and salt. Set aside.

In a medium-sized saucepan over a low heat, melt the butter with the chocolate, stirring occasionally until smooth. Remove from the heat and allow to cool for 5–10 minutes to lukewarm.

Meanwhile, beat the eggs with the sugar for 2–3 minutes until light and creamy. Add the vanilla and beat well. Add the chocolate mixture and beat until well combined. Add the dry ingredients and mix thoroughly. Stir in half of the pecans and half of the butterscotch chips. Spread the batter evenly in the prepared tin. Bake for 20 minutes. Remove from the oven and sprinkle the remaining pecans and butterscotch chips evenly over the brownie batter. Return to the oven and bake for a further 15–20 minutes or until a skewer inserted in the centre of the tin comes out with moist crumbs attached. Do not over-bake.

Allow to cool to room temperature or overnight before cutting and serving.

MAKES SIXTEEN 5-CM (2-IN) BROWNIES

Apricot Cream Cheese Streusel Bars

*T*his delicate bar combines a creamy filling with apricot preserves and a sweet crumb topping.

BASE
225 g (8 oz) unsalted butter, softened and cut into small pieces
250 g (9 oz) plain flour

CREAM CHEESE FILLING
225 g (8 oz) cream cheese (not softened)
65 g (2¼ oz) sugar
1 egg, at room temperature
1 teaspoon vanilla extract

STREUSEL TOPPING
185 g (6½ oz) plain flour
185 g (6½ oz) icing sugar
175 g (6 oz) unsalted butter, softened and cut into small pieces

APRICOT FILLING
240 g (8½ oz) apricot preserves (preferably unsweetened)

Preheat the oven to Gas Mark 4/180°C/fan oven 160°C.

To make the base, in a large bowl, using the medium speed of an electric mixer, beat together the butter and flour until crumbly and well combined. Transfer the mixture to an ungreased 33 x 23-cm (13 x 9-in) baking tin and, using your hands, pat the base firmly and evenly into the tin.

Bake the base for 15 minutes. Remove from the oven and allow to stand for about 45 minutes to cool completely.

To make the cream cheese filling, in a medium-sized bowl, using the medium speed of an electric mixer, beat together the cream cheese and sugar until smooth and creamy. Add the egg and vanilla and continue to beat until well combined. Set aside.

To make the streusel topping, in a medium-sized bowl, mix together the flour and sugar. Rub in the butter until the mixture resembles coarse crumbs, then toss until the ingredients are well combined. Set aside.

When the base is cool, spread the cream cheese filling evenly over it, leaving a 5-mm (¼-in) edge all around. Gently spread a thin layer of apricot filling over the cream cheese. Sprinkle the streusel topping over the entire top. Bake for 35 minutes. Cool to room temperature, cover tightly with cling film and allow to set overnight before cutting and serving.

MAKES TWENTY-FOUR 5-CM (2-IN) BARS

Coconut Pecan Shortbread Squares

This cookie bar has a simple shortbread base and layers of pecan nuts and coconut. It couldn't be easier to make – or more delicious.

Base

225 g (8 oz) unsalted butter, softened
    and cut into small pieces
250 g (9 oz) plain flour

Topping

225 g (8 oz) toasted pecan nuts,
    coarsely chopped (see Note)
175 g (6 oz) desiccated coconut
400 g (14 oz) canned sweetened
    condensed milk

Note: To toast the pecan nuts, place them on a baking tray in an oven at Gas Mark 4/180°C/ fan oven 160°C for 15 minutes or until lightly browned and fragrant.

Preheat the oven to Gas Mark 4/180°C/fan oven 160°C.

To make the base, in a large bowl, using the medium speed of an electric mixer, beat together the butter and flour until crumbly and well combined. Transfer the mixture to an ungreased 33 x 23-cm (13 x 9-in) baking tin and, using your hands, pat the base firmly and evenly into the tin. Bake for 15 minutes. Remove from the oven and allow to cool for 30 minutes.

Sprinkle the pecans and then the coconut over the base. Pour the condensed milk on top to completely cover the coconut. Use a spatula to spread it if necessary. Bake for 30–35 minutes or until lightly golden.

Cool to room temperature, cover tightly with cling film and allow to set overnight before cutting and serving.

Makes twenty-four 5-cm (2-in) squares

Hello Dolly Bars

After years of hearing customers and friends from the South tell me about a cookie bar that was just like the Magic Cookie Bar we serve at the bakery, I finally have received an actual recipe for Hello Dolly Bars from Maria Howard of Peculiar, Missouri. It turns out that the ingredients are a little different and they're even easier to make – you just add all the ingredients in a bowl and mix.

175 g (6 oz) digestive cookie crumbs
225 g (8 oz) pecan nuts, coarsely chopped
185 g (6 ½ oz) desiccated coconut
175 g (6 oz) plain chocolate chips

175 g (6 oz) butterscotch chips or white chocolate chips
175 g (6 oz) unsalted butter, melted
600 g (1 lb 5 oz) canned sweetened condensed milk

Preheat the oven to Gas Mark 3/160°C/fan oven 140°C.

Lightly grease a 33 x 23-cm (13 x 9-in) baking tin.

Mix together all the ingredients except the sweetened condensed milk in a large bowl. Transfer the mixture to the prepared tin and pat down evenly with your hands. Pour the sweetened condensed milk over the top to cover, using a spatula to spread if necessary. Bake for 30–35 minutes or until lightly golden. Cool to room temperature, cover tightly with cling film and allow to set overnight before cutting and serving.

MAKES TWENTY-FOUR 5-CM (2-IN) BARS

Chocolate Brownies with Caramel, Peanut Butter and Pecans

This is a variation on a brownie that we've been serving at the bakery for years. In this version, though, the caramel and pecan nuts, plus the surprisingly tasty addition of peanut butter chips, are layered between the cookie base and the brownie.

BASE
185 g (6½ oz) digestive cookie crumbs
175 g (6 oz) unsalted butter, melted

CARAMEL FILLING
450 g (1 lb) vanilla caramels
4 tablespoons double cream
85 g (3 oz) toasted pecan nuts,
    coarsely chopped (see Note)
85 g (3 oz) peanut butter chips or
    white chocolate chips

BROWNIE
65 g (2¼ oz) plain flour
¾ teaspoon baking powder
½ teaspoon salt
115 g (4 oz) unsalted butter
175 g (6 oz) plain chocolate
300 g (10½ oz) sugar
3 eggs, at room temperature
1 teaspoon vanilla extract

Note: To toast the pecan nuts, place them on a baking tray in an oven at Gas Mark 4/180°C/ fan oven 160°C for 15 minutes or until lightly browned and fragrant.

Preheat the oven to Gas Mark 4/180°C/fan oven 160°C.

To make the base, in a medium-sized bowl, combine the digestive cookies crumbs and melted butter. Press firmly into an ungreased 33 x 23-cm (13 x 9-in) baking tin. Set aside.

To make the caramel filling, in a medium-sized saucepan over low heat, melt the caramels with the cream, stirring occasionally, until smooth. Remove from the heat and pour over the cookie base. Use a spatula to spread it evenly. Sprinkle the pecans and peanut butter chips over the caramel. Set aside.

To make the brownie, in a small bowl, combine the flour, baking powder and salt. Set aside. In a medium-sized saucepan over low heat, melt the butter and chocolate, stirring occasionally until smooth. Remove from the heat, transfer to a large bowl and allow the mixture to cool for 5 minutes. Add the sugar, eggs and vanilla and beat well. Add the dry ingredients and mix thoroughly. Pour the batter over the pecans and peanut butter chips to completely cover the caramel layer. Bake for 35–45 minutes or until a skewer inserted in the centre of the tin comes out with moist crumbs attached. Do not over-bake.

Cool to room temperature, cover tightly with cling film and allow to set overnight before cutting and serving.

MAKES TWENTY-FOUR 5-CM (2-IN) BROWNIES

Shelly's Cherry Squares

This recipe comes from Shelly Sinko, who has been baking at Magnolia longer than anyone else. It's based on a cookie that her mum used to make when she was growing up.

115 g (4 oz) unsalted butter, softened
300 g (10½ oz) granulated sugar
4 eggs, at room temperature
1 teaspoon vanilla extract

250 g (9 oz) plain flour
125 g (4½ oz) canned cherry pie
    filling
icing sugar, for sprinkling

Preheat the oven to Gas Mark 4/180°C/fan oven 160°C.

Grease and lightly flour a 33 x 23-cm (13 x 9-in) baking tin.

In a large bowl, using the medium speed of an electric mixer, cream the butter with the granulated sugar for about 2 minutes until smooth. Add the eggs, one at a time, beating well after each addition. Add the vanilla. Add the flour and mix thoroughly.

Spread the dough evenly in the prepared tin. With a small, sharp knife, score into twenty-four 5-cm (2-in) squares.

Place a teaspoon of cherry pie filling (each containing one cherry) on each scored square. Bake for 30–35 minutes or until a skewer inserted in the centre of the tin comes out clean.

Allow to cool to room temperature, then sprinkle generously with icing sugar before cutting and serving.

MAKES TWENTY-FOUR 5-CM (2-IN) SQUARES

Blondies with White and Plain Chocolate Chunks

A moist and chewy butterscotch bar with two kinds of chocolate and lots of walnuts.

200 g (7 oz) superfine plain flour
1 teaspoon baking powder
¼ teaspoon salt
175 g (6 oz) unsalted butter, softened
225 g (8 oz) light brown sugar
100 g (3½ oz) granulated sugar
2 eggs, at room temperature

2 teaspoons vanilla extract
125 g (4½ oz) walnuts, coarsely chopped
125 g (4½ oz) white chocolate, coarsely chopped
85 g (3 oz) plain chocolate, coarsely chopped

Preheat the oven to Gas Mark 4/180°C/fan oven 160°C.

Grease and lightly flour a 33 x 23-cm (13 x 9-in) baking tin.

In a small bowl, combine the flour, baking powder and salt. Set aside.

In a large bowl, cream the butter with the sugars for about 2 minutes until smooth. Add the eggs and vanilla and beat well. Add the dry ingredients and mix thoroughly. Stir in the walnuts and chocolate chunks. Spread the batter evenly in the prepared tin. Bake for 35–40 minutes or until a skewer inserted in the centre of the tin comes out with moist crumbs attached. Do not over-bake.

Allow to cool to room temperature or overnight before cutting and serving.

MAKES TWENTY-FOUR 5-CM (2-IN) BLONDIES

Pumpkin Bars
with Cream Cheese Icing

We start making these bars at the bakery during the week of Halloween. And every year both the customers and the staff can hardly wait that long. They're very, very good.

BARS
185 g (6½ oz) plain flour
1½ teaspoons baking powder
1½ teaspoons cinnamon
1 teaspoon bicarbonate of soda
¼ teaspoon salt
285 g (10 oz) canned pumpkin purée
225 g (8 oz) sugar
175 ml (6 fl oz) vegetable oil
   (preferably rapeseed)
3 eggs, at room temperature

55 g (2 oz) toasted pecan nuts,
   coarsely chopped (see Note)

ICING
½ recipe Cream Cheese Icing (page 118)

DECORATION
55 g (2 oz) toasted pecan nuts,
   coarsely chopped (see Note)

Note: To toast the pecan nuts, place them on a baking tray in a Gas Mark 4/180°C/ fan oven 160°C oven for 15 minutes or until lightly browned and fragrant.

Preheat the oven to Gas Mark 4/180°C/fan oven 160°C.

Grease and lightly flour a 33 x 23-cm (13 x 9-in) baking tin.

To make the bars, in a small bowl, sift together the flour, baking powder, cinnamon, bicarbonate of soda and salt. Set aside.

In a large bowl, using the medium speed of an electric mixer, beat together the pumpkin, sugar, oil and eggs for about 3 minutes until smooth. Add the dry ingredients and mix thoroughly. Stir in the pecans. Pour the batter into the prepared tin. Bake for 25–30 minutes or until a skewer inserted in the centre of the tin comes out clean.

Remove from the oven and allow to cool completely before icing the top with the Cream Cheese Icing. Decorate with pecans as desired before cutting and serving.

MAKES TWELVE 7.5CM (3-INCH) BARS

Pies and Tarts

Apple Tart with
Hazelnut Brown Sugar Topping

*T*his tart is a nice alternative to apple pie and it makes a great dessert for a dinner party, especially if served with vanilla ice cream and perhaps some caramel sauce.

BROWN SUGAR TOPPING

100 g (3 ½ oz) plain flour
115 g (4 oz) light brown sugar
85 g (3 oz) unsalted butter, softened
    and cut into small pieces
55 g (2 oz) hazelnuts, coarsely chopped

FILLING

325 g (11 ½ oz) thinly sliced tart apples
65 g (2 ¼ oz) sugar

1 tablespoon flour
1 teaspoon vanilla extract

PASTRY

85 g (3 oz) unsalted butter, softened
2 tablespoons sugar
1 egg, at room temperature
1 egg yolk, at room temperature
185 g (6 ½ oz) plain flour
1 tablespoon baking powder

Preheat the oven to Gas Mark 3/160°C/fan oven 140°C.

To make the topping, in a medium-sized bowl, mix together the flour and sugar. Rub in the butter until the mixture resembles coarse crumbs. Add the hazelnuts and toss until all the ingredients are well combined. Set aside.

To make the filling, place all the ingredients in a large bowl and toss gently until the fruit is evenly coated. Set aside.

To make the pastry, in a large bowl, on the low speed of an electric mixer, cream the butter and sugar until smooth. Add the egg and egg yolk and mix well. Add the flour and baking powder and beat until just combined. Gather the dough into a ball and on a lightly floured surface roll it out to fit a 25-cm (10-in) tart tin. Fit the dough into the tin and trim the edge flush with the rim of the tin.

Transfer the fruit filling into the pastry case and sprinkle the brown sugar topping evenly over the fruit. Place the tart on a baking tray and bake for 50 minutes.

Cool on a wire rack for 1–2 hours. Serve warm or at room temperature.

MAKES ONE 25-CM (10-IN) TART

Strawberry Pie

A few summers ago I was searching for a good strawberry pie recipe and realised that all the recipes I could find called for a pre-baked pie case, a filling made on the hob and then a chilling period in the refrigerator. I really wanted to make a regular bake-in-the-oven strawberry pie with a pastry lid – and, with the right amount of tapioca to balance the juiciness of the berries, you can.

FILLING
850 g (1 lb 14 oz) fresh strawberries, sliced in half
100 g (3½ oz) sugar
40 g (1½ oz) quick-cooking tapioca
1 teaspoon vanilla extract

PASTRY
285 g (10 oz) plain flour
200 g (7 oz) vegetable fat, diced
6 tablespoons ice water

GLAZE
1 tablespoon milk
1 tablespoon sugar

Preheat the oven to Gas Mark 6/200°C/fan oven 190°C.

To make the filling, place all the ingredients in a large bowl and toss gently until the fruit is evenly coated. Leave to stand for 15 minutes while preparing the pastry.

To make the pastry, place the flour in a large bowl and rub in the vegetable fat until the pieces are pea-sized. Sprinkle the ice water by tablespoonfuls over the flour mixture and toss with a fork until all the dough is moistened. Gather the dough into a ball, separate into two pieces and wrap one piece in greaseproof paper and set aside. Roll out the first piece on a lightly floured surface to fit a 23-cm (9-in) glass pie dish and trim, leaving 1 cm (½ in) around the edge.

Transfer the fruit filling into the pastry case. Unwrap the reserved piece of dough, roll it out to form the lid and trim to fit. Fold the 1-cm (½-in) excess on the pastry case over the edge of the lid. Seal by crimping the edges together. Brush the lid with the milk, then sprinkle evenly with the sugar. Make several 2.5-cm (1-in) steam slits in the centre of the pie with the tip of a paring knife. Place the pie on a baking tray, lower the oven temperature to Gas Mark 4/180°C/fan oven 160°C and bake for 60–70 minutes, until the pastry is golden.

Cool on a wire rack for at least 2 hours. Serve warm or at room temperature, with sweetened whipped cream, if desired.

MAKES ONE 23-CM (9-IN) PIE

Nancy's Prize-winning Blueberry Pie

This recipe comes from Nancy Schatz of Augusta, Maine. The pie won first prize in the 1991 Old Hallowell Day bake-off.

PASTRY

310 g (11 oz) plain flour
3 tablespoons sugar
1 teaspoon salt
55 g (2 oz) unsalted butter, chilled and cut into small pieces
40 g (1 ½ oz) vegetable fat, chilled and cut into small pieces
5 tablespoons orange juice (use a variety without the bits)

FILLING

425 g (15 oz) fresh blueberries
200 g (7 oz) sugar
25 g (1 oz) quick-cooking tapioca
3 tablespoons brandy
2 tablespoons freshly squeezed lemon juice
¼ teaspoon cinnamon
25 g (1 oz) unsalted butter, chilled and cut into small pieces

To make the pastry, place the flour, sugar and salt in a large bowl. Rub in the butter and vegetable fat until the pieces are pea-sized. Sprinkle the orange juice by tablespoonfuls over the flour mixture and toss with a fork until all the dough is moistened. Gather the dough into a ball and separate into two pieces. Wrap the pieces tightly with cling film and refrigerate for 30 minutes. Five minutes before removing the chilled pie dough from the refrigerator, prepare your filling.

To make the filling, in a large bowl, place the berries, sugar, tapioca, brandy, lemon juice and cinnamon. Toss gently until the fruit is evenly coated. Allow to stand for 15 minutes while rolling out the dough.

Preheat the oven to Gas Mark 7/220°C/fan oven 200°C.

On a lightly floured surface, roll out half of the dough to fit a 23-cm (9-in) glass pie dish and trim, leaving 1 cm (½ in) around the edge. Transfer the fruit filling into the pastry case, mounding it in the centre. Dot with the butter.

Roll out the pastry lid and trim it to fit, folding the 1-cm (½-in) excess on the pastry case over the edge of the lid. Seal by crimping the edges together. Make several 2.5-cm (1-in) steam slits in the centre of the pie with the tip of a paring knife. Place the pie on a baking tray and bake for 15 minutes. Lower the oven temperature to Gas Mark 4/180°C/fan oven 160°C and continue baking for a further 30 minutes.

Cool on a wire rack for at least 2 hours before serving.

MAKES ONE 23-CM (9-IN) PIE

Chocolate Pecan Pudding Pie

I have this wonderful childhood memory of a pie that had a custardy chocolate filling with pecan nuts that wasn't like the standard chocolate pecan pie, which I usually find too rich and sweet. This recipe combines our chocolate pudding from the bakery with pecans and pastry – a simple old-fashioned dessert that comes pretty close to my memory.

PASTRY
150 g (5 oz) plain flour
100 g (3½ oz) vegetable fat
3 tablespoons ice water

FILLING
200 g (7 oz) sugar
40 g (1½ oz) cocoa powder
30 g (1¼ oz) cornflour
Pinch of salt
700 ml (1¼ pints) milk

175 g (6 oz) toasted pecan nuts,
    coarsely chopped (see Note)
1 tablespoon vanilla extract

DECORATION
Sweetened whipped cream
Toasted pecan nuts, coarsely chopped

Note: To toast the pecan nuts, place them on a baking tray in an oven at Gas Mark 4/180°C/ fan oven 160°C for 15 minutes or until lightly browned and fragrant.

Preheat the oven to Gas Mark 7/220°C/fan oven 200°C.

To make the pastry, place the flour in a large bowl and rub in the vegetable fat until the pieces are pea-sized. Sprinkle the ice water by tablespoonfuls over the flour mixture and toss with a fork until all the dough is moistened. Gather the dough into a ball and roll out on a lightly floured surface to fit a 23-cm (9-in) glass pie dish and trim, leaving 1 cm (½ in) around the edge. Fold the edges under all around the rim and crimp. Prick all over the base and sides of the pastry case with a fork. Place the pie dish on a baking tray and bake for 20–25 minutes or until the edges of the pastry are lightly golden. Remove from the oven and allow to stand for about 45 minutes to cool to room temperature.

To make the filling, in a medium-sized saucepan, combine the sugar, cocoa, cornflour and salt. Add the milk and whisk over a medium heat for about 15 minutes until the pudding thickens and begins to bubble. Remove from the heat and stir in the pecans and vanilla. Pour immediately into the cooled pastry case. Cover the top of the pie with greaseproof paper to prevent a skin forming and cool for 30 minutes.

Remove the greaseproof paper, cover the pie tightly with cling film and refrigerate for at least 3 hours or overnight. Serve with sweetened whipped cream and then decorate with the pecans.

MAKES ONE 23-CM (9-IN) PIE

Nectarine Pie

*N*o one ever seems to make nectarine pie and I'm not sure why. I adore nectarines (possibly even more than peaches) and this is one of my favourite summertime desserts to make when nectarines are perfectly ripe and in season.

FILLING
800 g (1 lb 11 oz) ripe nectarines, sliced (see Note)
100 g (3½ oz) granulated sugar
115 g (4 oz) soft light brown sugar
40 g (1½ oz) quick-cooking tapioca
1 teaspoon vanilla extract

PASTRY
285 g (10 oz) plain flour
20 g (7 oz) vegetable fat, cut into small pieces
6 tablespoons ice water

GLAZE
1 tablespoon milk
1 tablespoon sugar

Note: Make sure to blanch the nectarines in boiling water for 60 seconds, transfer to an ice water bath and remove the skins before slicing.

Preheat the oven to Gas Mark 6/200°C/fan oven 180°C.

To make the filling, place all the ingredients in a large bowl and toss gently until the fruit is evenly coated. Leave to stand for 15 minutes while preparing the pastry.

To make the pastry, place the flour in a large bowl and rub in the vegetable fat until the pieces are pea-sized. Sprinkle the ice water by tablespoonfuls over the flour mixture and toss with a fork until all the dough is moistened. Gather the dough into a ball and separate into two pieces. Wrap one piece in greaseproof paper and set aside. Roll out the first piece on a lightly floured surface to fit a 23-cm (9-in) glass pie dish and trim, leaving 1 cm (½ in) around the edge.

Transfer the fruit filling into the pastry case. Unwrap the reserved piece of dough, roll it out as the pastry lid and trim to fit. Fold the 1-cm (½-in) excess on the pastry case over the edge of the pastry lid. Seal by crimping the edges together. Brush the lid with the milk, then sprinkle evenly with the sugar. Make several 2.5-cm (1-in) steam slits in the centre of the pie with the tip of a paring knife. Place the pie on a baking tray, lower the oven temperature to Gas Mark 4/180°C/fan oven 160°C and bake for 60–70 minutes until the crust is golden.

Cool on a wire rack for at least 2 hours. Serve warm or at room temperature with sweetened whipped cream if wished.

MAKES ONE 23-CM (9-IN) PIE

Plum Tart with Almond Streusel Topping

I had never really given much thought to baking with plums until my friend Kate had us over for dinner one evening and served a plum galette for dessert. I went right out to the market, got some plums and started experimenting. Make sure you use ripe, flavourful plums for this tart.

STREUSEL TOPPING
100 g (3½ oz) plain flour
150 g (5 oz) sugar
85 g (3 oz) unsalted butter, softened
   and cut into small pieces
65 g (2¼ oz) toasted almonds,
   chopped (see Note)

FILLING
500 g (1 lb 2 oz) plums, thinly sliced
50 g (1¾ oz) sugar

1 tablespoon plain flour
1 teaspoon vanilla extract

PASTRY
85 g (3 oz) unsalted butter, softened
2 tablespoons sugar
1 egg, at room temperature
1 egg yolk, at room temperature
185 g (6½ oz) plain flour
1 tablespoon baking powder

Note: To toast the almonds, place them on a baking tray in an oven at Gas Mark 4/180°C/ fan oven 160°C for 15 minutes or until lightly browned and fragrant.

Preheat the oven to Gas Mark 3/160°C/fan oven 140°C.

To make the topping, in a medium-sized bowl, mix together the flour and sugar. Rub in the butter until the mixture resembles coarse crumbs. Add the almonds and toss until all the ingredients are well combined. Set aside.

To make the filling, place all the ingredients in a large bowl and toss gently until the fruit is evenly coated. Set aside.

To make the pastry, in a large bowl, using the low speed of an electric mixer, cream the butter and sugar until smooth. Add the egg and egg yolk and mix well. Add the flour and baking powder and beat until just combined. Gather the dough into a ball and roll it out on a lightly floured surface to fit a 25-cm (10-in) tart tin. Fit the dough into the tin and trim the edge flush with the rim of the tin.

Transfer the fruit filling into the pastry case and sprinkle the streusel topping evenly over the fruit. Place the tart on a baking tray and bake for 45 minutes.

Cool on a wire rack for 1–2 hours. Serve warm or at room temperature with sweetened whipped cream if wished.

MAKES ONE 25-CM (10-IN) TART

Jill's Apple Pie

*T*his is my friend Jill Rowe's favourite apple pie recipe. It was the most popular dessert that she made when she owned and ran a local restaurant, The Kitchen, near my home in upstate New York.

PASTRY

250 g (9 oz) plain flour
½ teaspoon salt
150 g (5 oz) vegetable fat, chilled and
    cut into small pieces
55 g (2 oz) unsalted butter, chilled
    and cut into small pieces
5 tablespoons ice water

FILLING

150 g (5 oz) sugar
2 tablespoons plain flour
½ teaspoon cinnamon
⅛ teaspoon nutmeg
⅛ teaspoon salt
625 g (1 lb 6 oz) sliced tart green
    apples (preferably Granny Smith)
55 g (2 oz) unsalted butter, chilled
    and cut into small pieces

To make the pastry, place the flour and salt in a large bowl and rub in the vegetable fat and butter until the pieces are pea-sized. Sprinkle the ice water by tablespoonfuls over the flour mixture and toss with a fork until all the dough is moistened. Gather the dough into a ball and separate into two pieces. Wrap the pieces tightly with cling film and refrigerate for 30 minutes.

Preheat the oven to Gas Mark 6/200°C/fan oven 180°C.

To make the filling, place the sugar, flour, cinnamon, nutmeg and salt in a large bowl. Add the apples and toss gently until the fruit is evenly coated.

Roll out one piece of the dough on a lightly floured surface to fit a 23-cm (9-in) glass pie dish and trim, leaving 1 cm (½ in) around the edge. Transfer the fruit filling into the pastry case, mounding it in the centre. Dot with the butter.

Roll out the second piece of dough into a pastry lid and trim to fit. Fold the 1-cm (½-in) excess on the pastry case over the edge of the pastry lid. Seal by crimping the edges together. Make several 2.5-cm (1-in) steam slits in the centre of the pie with the tip of a paring knife. Place the pie on a baking tray and bake for 50 minutes.

Cool on a wire rack for at least 2 hours. Serve warm or at room temperature with sweetened whipped cream if wished.

Pumpkin Pie

I think we all have our favourite pumpkin pie recipe. This is my latest version – not too spicy and with a hint of bourbon.

PASTRY
150 g (5 oz) plain flour
100 g (3½ oz) vegetable fat
3 tablespoons ice water

FILLING
425 g (15 oz) canned pumpkin purée
2 eggs, at room temperature

100 g (3½ oz) granulated sugar
55 g (2 oz) soft light brown sugar
1 teaspoon cinnamon
½ teaspoon mixed spice
¼ teaspoon salt
300 ml (10 fl oz) evaporated milk
3 tablespoons bourbon

Preheat the oven to Gas Mark 7/220°C/fan oven 200°C.

To make the pastry, place the flour in a large bowl and rub in the vegetable fat until the pieces are pea-sized. Sprinkle the ice water by tablespoonfuls over the flour mixture and toss with a fork until all the dough is moistened. Gather the dough into a ball, roll out on a lightly floured surface to fit a 23-cm (9-in) glass pie dish and trim, leaving 1 cm (½ in) around the edge. Fold the edges under all around the rim and crimp. Set aside.

To make the filling, in a large bowl, using the medium speed of an electric mixer, combine the pumpkin and eggs and beat well. Add the sugars, cinnamon, mixed spice and salt and mix until well combined. Combine the evaporated milk and bourbon and stir into the pumpkin mixture in three parts.

Pour the filling into the prepared pastry case. Place the pie on a baking tray and bake for 15 minutes. Lower the oven temperature to Gas Mark 4/180°C/ fan oven 160°C and continue baking for a further 50–60 minutes or until a skewer inserted in the centre of the pie comes out clean. Cool on a wire rack for at least 2 hours.

Serve warm or at room temperature with sweetened whipped cream if wished.

MAKES ONE 23-CM (9-IN) PIE

Cheese Pies
and
Cheesecakes

Strawberry Cream Cheese Pie with a Cookie Base

At the farmers market near my house every summer, there is a woman who grows and sells the most perfect half-wild strawberries I have ever eaten. The first ones we eat straight out of the punnet and with the second I make this great cream cheese pie.

BASE
115 g (4 oz) unsalted butter, melted
125 g (4½ oz) digestive cookie crumbs
55 g (2 oz) toasted pecan nuts,
    chopped (see Note)
50 g (1¾ oz) soft light brown sugar

FILLING
450 g (1 lb) cream cheese, softened
125 g (4½ oz) icing sugar
4 tablespoons sour cream
1 teaspoon vanilla extract

TOPPING
325 g (11½ oz) fresh strawberries,
    sliced in half

Note: To toast the pecan nuts, place them on a baking tray in an oven at Gas Mark 4/180°C/ fan oven 160°C for 15 minutes or until lightly browned and fragrant.

Preheat the oven to Gas Mark 4/180°C/fan oven 160°C.

To make the base, in a medium-sized bowl, combine the butter with the cookie crumbs, pecans and sugar. Press firmly into a lightly buttered 23-cm (9-in) glass pie dish. Place on a baking tray and bake for 12 minutes. Remove from the oven and allow to cool on a wire rack.

To make the filling, in a large bowl, using the low speed of an electric mixer, beat together the cream cheese and sugar until smooth and creamy. Add the sour cream and vanilla and continue to beat on a low speed until well combined.

Refrigerate the filling while the base is cooling. When the base is completely cooled, spread the filling evenly over it with a rubber spatula. Arrange the sliced strawberries on top of the filling in a decorative manner.

Refrigerate the pie for at least 8 hours or overnight to ensure that the filling sets.

MAKES ONE 23-CM (9-IN) PIE

Caramel Apple Pecan Cheesecake

*E*very Thanksgiving at my cousin Polly's house we gather the evening before to do the holiday baking, and every year I am called upon to create a new cheesecake. This is last year's recipe and it was loved by all.

PASTRY
150 g (5 oz) superfine plain flour
55 g (2 oz) soft light brown sugar
115 g (4 oz) unsalted butter, softened
    and cut into small pieces
115 (4 oz) toasted pecan nuts,
    chopped (see Note)

FILLING
900 g (2 lb) cream cheese, softened
160 g (5½ oz) sugar
5 eggs, at room temperature
2 tablespoons double cream
1 tablespoon vanilla extract

APPLE TOPPING
275 g (9½ oz) thinly sliced tart apples
    (such as Granny Smith)
50 g (1¾ oz) sugar
⅛ teaspoon cinnamon
25 g (1 oz) unsalted butter

DECORATION
150 ml (5 fl oz) Caramel Sauce (page
    124)
40 g (1½ oz) toasted pecan nuts,
    coarsely chopped (see Note)

Note: To toast the pecan nuts, place them on a baking tray in an oven at Gas Mark 4/180°C/ fan oven 160°C for 15 minutes or until lightly browned and fragrant.

Preheat the oven to Gas Mark 4/180°C/fan oven 160°C.

    To make the pastry, in a large bowl, mix together the flour and sugar. Rub in the butter until the mixture resembles coarse crumbs. Add the pecans and toss until all the ingredients are well combined. Press into the base of a buttered 25-cm (10-in) springform tin. Bake for 20 minutes.

Remove from the oven and allow to cool on a wire rack. Lower the oven temperature to Gas Mark 3/160°C/fan oven 140°C.

To make the filling, in a large bowl, using the low speed of an electric mixer, beat the cream cheese until very smooth. Gradually add the sugar. Add the eggs, one at a time. To ensure that the filling has no lumps and that no ingredients stick to the base of the bowl, stop the mixer several times and scrape down the sides of the bowl with a rubber spatula. Stir in the double cream and vanilla.

Pour the filling into the pastry case and set the tin on a baking tray. Bake for about 1 hour until the edges are set and the centre moves only slightly when the tin is shaken. At the end of the baking time, turn off the heat and, using a wooden spoon to keep the oven door slightly ajar, allow the cake to cool in the oven for 1 hour before removing. Cover and refrigerate for at least 12 hours or overnight.

To make the apple topping, toss the apples with the sugar and cinnamon. In a medium-sized saucepan, melt the butter over a medium-high heat. Add the apples and cook, stirring occasionally, for 8–10 minutes until the apples are very soft and easily pierced with a fork. Remove the apples from the heat, transfer them to a small bowl and allow to stand for about 45 minutes to cool to room temperature. When the apples have cooled, spread them evenly in a thin layer over the top of the cheesecake. Return the cake to the refrigerator.

Remove the cake from the refrigerator 15–30 minutes before cutting and serving. To decorate, drizzle the Caramel over the apples and then sprinkle with the pecans.

MAKES ONE 25-CM (10-IN) CHEESECAKE

Cream Cheese Pecan Pie

This is one of my favourite new pie recipes. The surprising combination of the cream cheese filling with the standard pecan pie filling is quite delicious.

CREAM CHEESE FILLING
225 g (8 oz) cream cheese (not softened)
40 g (1½ oz) sugar
1 egg, at room temperature
1 teaspoon vanilla extract
¼ teaspoon salt

SYRUP FILLING
3 eggs, at room temperature
225 g (8 oz) golden syrup

55 g (2 oz) soft light brown sugar
1 teaspoon vanilla extract

PASTRY CASE
150 g (5 oz) plain flour
100 g (3½ oz) vegetable fat
3 tablespoons ice water

150 g (5 oz) toasted pecan nuts, coarsely chopped (see Note)

Note: To toast the pecan nuts, place them on a baking tray in an oven at Gas Mark 4/180°C/ fan oven 160°C for 15 minutes or until lightly browned and fragrant.

Preheat the oven to Gas Mark 5/190°C/fan oven 170°C.

To make the cream cheese filling, in a medium-sized bowl, using the medium speed of an electric mixer, beat together the cream cheese and sugar until smooth and creamy. Add the egg, vanilla and salt, continuing to beat for 3–5 minutes until the ingredients are well blended and the mixture is considerably thicker. (I recommend using the whisk attachment if your mixer has one.) Set aside.

To make the syrup filling, in a small bowl, using the medium speed of an electric mixer, beat the eggs for 1 minute. Add the golden syrup, sugar and vanilla and beat for a further 1 minute. Set aside.

To make the pastry case, place the flour in a large bowl and rub in the vegetable fat until the pieces are pea-sized. Sprinkle the ice water by tablespoonfuls over the flour mixture and toss with a fork until all the dough is moistened. Gather the dough into a ball and roll it out on a lightly floured surface to fit a 23-cm (9-in) glass pie dish and trim, leaving 1 cm (½ in) around the edge. Fold the edges under all around the rim and crimp.

Spread the cream cheese filling evenly in the pastry case. Sprinkle with the pecans. Slowly and carefully pour the syrup filling over the pecans. Place the pie on a baking tray and bake for 50–60 minutes, or until the centre of the pie is set.

Cool on a wire rack for at least 4 hours before cutting and serving. This pie is best served at room temperature, not warm, with sweetened whipped cream.

MAKES ONE 23-CM (9-IN) PIE

Pumpkin Cheesecake
with a Ginger Nut Pecan Base

This cheesecake has been a huge success at the bakery since its introduction. It is a lovely dessert for an autumn dinner party. I love to make cheesecakes when I'm entertaining because they can be made one to two days in advance, before the guests even arrive.

Base
115 g (4 oz) unsalted butter, melted
125 g (4½ oz) ginger nut cookie
   crumbs
55 g (2 oz) toasted pecan nuts,
   chopped (see Note)

Filling
350 g (12 oz) cream cheese, softened
150 g (5 oz) granulated sugar
160 g (5½ oz) soft brown sugar

5 eggs, at room temperature
350 g (12 oz) canned pumpkin purée
175 ml (6 fl oz) double cream
1½ teaspoons cinnamon

Decoration
Sweet Vanilla Whipped Cream (see
   page 121)
Toasted pecan nut halves (see Note)

Note: To toast the pecan nuts, place them on a baking tray in an oven at Gas Mark 4/180°C/fan oven 160°C oven for 15 minutes or until lightly browned and fragrant.

Preheat the oven to Gas Mark 3/160°C/fan oven 140°C.

To make the base, in a small bowl, combine the butter with the cookie crumbs and pecans. Press into the base of a buttered 25-cm (10-in) springform tin. Bake for 10 minutes. Remove from the oven and allow to cool on a wire rack.

To make the filling, in a large bowl, using the low speed of an electric mixer, beat the cream cheese until very smooth. Gradually add the sugars. Add the eggs, one at a time. Add the pumpkin purée and mix until just blended. To ensure that the batter has no lumps and that no ingredients stick to the base of the bowl, stop the mixer several times and scrape down the sides of the bowl with a rubber spatula. Stir in the double cream and cinnamon.

Pour the filling into the prepared base and set the tin on a baking tray. Bake for about 1 hour until the edges are set and the centre moves only slightly when the tin is shaken. At the end of the baking time, turn off the heat and, using a wooden spoon to keep the oven door slightly ajar, cool the cake in the oven for 1 hour before removing. Cover and refrigerate for at least 12 hours or overnight.

Remove the cake from the refrigerator 15–30 minutes before cutting and serving. Decorate with the Sweet Vanilla Whipped Cream and toasted pecan halves.

MAKES ONE 25-CM (10-IN) CHEESECAKE

Peaches and Cream Pie

*T*his is a lovely, light summertime dessert that you should make only when you have peaches that are perfectly ripe and sweet.

PASTRY
115 g (4 oz) unsalted butter, softened
3 tablespoons sugar
1 egg yolk, at room temperature
3 tablespoons double cream
185 g (6½ oz) plain flour
¼ teaspoon salt

FILLING
450 g (1 lb) cream cheese, softened
185 g (6½ oz) icing sugar
125 ml (4 fl oz) double cream
2 teaspoons vanilla extract

TOPPING
450 g (1 lb) ripe peaches, thinly sliced
(see Note)

Note: Make sure you blanch the peaches in boiling water for 60 seconds, transfer to an ice water bath and remove the skins before slicing.

Preheat the oven to Gas Mark 5/190°C/fan oven 170°C.

To make the pastry, in a large bowl, using the low speed of an electric mixer, cream the butter and sugar until smooth. Add the egg yolk and cream and mix well. Add the flour and salt and beat until just combined. Gather the dough into a ball and roll it out on a lightly floured surface to fit into a 23-cm (9-in) glass pie dish. Fold the edges under all around the rim and crimp. Prick the base and sides all over with the tines of a fork. Cover the edge of the pastry case with kitchen foil, place on a baking tray and bake for 10 minutes. Carefully remove the foil and continue baking for a further 20 minutes, until the pastry is crisp and golden. Remove from the oven and allow to cool on a wire rack.

To make the filling, in a large bowl, using the low speed of an electric mixer, beat together the cream cheese and sugar until smooth and creamy. Add the double cream and vanilla and continue to beat on a low speed until well combined.

Refrigerate the filling while the pastry case is cooling. When completely cooled, spread the filling evenly in the pastry case with a rubber spatula. Arrange the sliced peaches on top of the filling in a decorative manner.

Refrigerate the pie for at least 8 hours or overnight to ensure that the filling sets.

MAKES ONE 23-CM (9-IN) PIE

Coconut Pecan Cheesecake

*T*his year's Thanksgiving cheesecake recipe . . .

Base
115 g (4 oz) unsalted butter, melted
100 g (3 ½ oz) digestive cookie
   crumbs
55 g (2 oz) toasted pecan nuts,
   chopped (see Note)
50 g (1 ¾ oz) sugar

Filling
900 g (2 lb) cream cheese, softened
200 g (7 oz) sugar

5 eggs, at room temperature
150 g (5 oz) desiccated coconut
2 tablespoons double cream
2 teaspoons vanilla extract
1 teaspoon coconut extract

Decoration
50 g (1 ¾ oz) desiccated coconut
30 g (1 ¼ oz) toasted pecan nuts,
   chopped (see Note)

*N*ote: To toast the pecan nuts, place them on a baking tray in an oven at Gas Mark 4/180°C/ fan oven 160°C for 15 minutes or until lightly browned and fragrant.

Preheat the oven to Gas Mark 3/160°C/fan oven 140°C.

To make the base, in a small bowl, combine the butter with the cookie crumbs, pecans and sugar. Press into the base of a buttered 25-cm (10-in) springform tin. Bake for 10 minutes. Remove from the oven and allow to cool on a wire rack.

To make the filling, in a large bowl, using the low speed of an electric mixer, beat the cream cheese until very smooth. Gradually add the sugar. Add the eggs, one at a time. To ensure that the batter has no lumps and that no ingredients stick to the base of the bowl, stop the mixer several times and scrape down the sides of the bowl with a rubber spatula. Stir in the coconut, double cream and vanilla and coconut extracts.

(cont.)

*M*agnolia's Vanilla and Chocolate Cupcakes
with Vanilla Buttercream

$\mathcal{R}$ed Velvet Cake with Creamy Vanilla Icing

*P*umpkin Cheesecake with a Ginger Pecan Base

Raspberry Cream Cheese Breakfast Buns,
Nectarine Pie,
Vanilla Cake with Vanilla Buttercream,
Chocolate Cake with Vanilla Buttercream

Vanilla Layer Creme Cookie Ice Cream,
White Chocolate Peanut Brittle Ice Cream,
Old-fashioned Chocolate Chip Ice Cream

*a*pple Tart with Hazelnut Brown Sugar Topping

IN THE JARS: Coconut Oatmeal Drop Cookies, Chocolate Chocolate Chip Drop Cookies,
Peanut Butter Chocolate Chip Pecan Cookies

ON THE CAKE STAND: Iced Ginger Cookies, White Chocolate Pecan Drop Cookies,
Blondies with Cream Cheese Swirl and Pecans

ON THE PLATE: Coconut Pecan Shortbread Squares,
Chocolate Fudge Brownies with Butterscotch Chips and Pecans,
White Chocolate Pecan Drop Cookies

$\mathcal{D}$evil's Food Cake with Seven-minute Icing and Coconut

Pour the filling into the prepared tin and set the tin on a baking tray. Bake for about 1 hour until the edges are set and the centre moves only slightly when the tin is shaken. At the end of the baking time, turn off the heat and, using a wooden spoon to keep the oven door slightly ajar, cool the cake in the oven for 1 hour before removing. Cover and refrigerate for at least 12 hours or overnight.

Remove the cake from the refrigerator 15–30 minutes before cutting and serving. To decorate, sprinkle the coconut and pecans around the top edge of the cake.

MAKES ONE 25-CM (10-IN) CHEESECAKE

Cupcakes and Layer Cakes

Black Bottom Cupcakes

*D*uring my quest in the kitchen for the perfect version of one of my favourite childhood treats, I was surprised to discover that many of my friends and neighbours (that is, testers) had never tried a black bottom cupcake before. If you're part of this group, you need to bake a batch – they're absolutely wonderful.

CREAM CHEESE FILLING
350 g (12 oz) cream cheese (not
     softened)
100 g (3½ oz) sugar
1 egg, at room temperature
55 g (2 oz) miniature plain chocolate
     chips

CUPCAKES
215 g (7½ oz) plain flour
65 g (2¼ oz) cocoa powder
1 teaspoon bicarbonate of soda
¼ teaspoon salt
125 ml (4 fl oz) vegetable oil (preferably
     rapeseed)
200 g (7 oz) sugar
250 ml (9 fl oz) buttermilk
2 teaspoons vanilla extract

Preheat the oven to Gas Mark 4/180°C/fan oven 160°C.

Line two 12-hole muffin tins with 18 cupcake paper cases.

To make the cream cheese filling, in a medium-sized bowl, beat the cream cheese and sugar until smooth. Add the egg and beat well. Stir in the chocolate chips. Set aside.

To make the cupcakes, in a small bowl, combine the flour, cocoa, bicarbonate of soda and salt. Set aside. In a large bowl, using the medium speed of an electric mixer, beat together the oil and sugar. Add the dry ingredients in two parts, alternating with the buttermilk and vanilla and making sure all ingredients are well blended. Carefully spoon the cupcake batter into the cupcake cases, filling them about two-thirds full. Drop a small scoop (about 1½ tablespoons) of the cream cheese filling on top of each cupcake. Bake for 30–35 minutes or until a skewer inserted in the centre comes out clean.

Cool the cupcakes in the tins for 30 minutes. Remove from the tins and cool completely on a wire rack.

MAKES 18 CUPCAKES

Strawberry Shortcake

Here is an old-fashioned favourite that doesn't seem to go out of style. I recommend serving this cake relatively soon after assembling it, since the whipped cream tends to melt a little in warm weather. I never refrigerate cakes because they dry out quickly when chilled.

CAKE

185 g (6½ oz) self-raising flour
160 g (5½ oz) plain flour
225 g (8 oz) unsalted butter, softened
400 g (14 oz) sugar
4 eggs, at room temperature
250 ml (9 fl oz) milk
1 teaspoon vanilla extract

CREAM FILLING

475 ml (17 fl oz) double cream
30 g (1¼ oz) icing sugar
2 teaspoons vanilla extract

STRAWBERRY FILLING

285 g (10 oz) ripe strawberries, sliced in half
2 tablespoons sugar

Preheat the oven to Gas Mark 4/180°C/fan oven 160°C.

Grease and lightly flour three 23 x 5-cm (9 x 2-in) round cake tins, then base-line with greaseproof paper.

To make the cake, in a small bowl, combine the flours and set aside. In a large bowl, using the medium speed of an electric mixer, cream the butter until smooth. Add the sugar gradually and beat for about 3 minutes until fluffy. Add the eggs, one at a time, beating well after each addition. Add the dry ingredients in three parts, alternating with the milk and vanilla. With each addition, beat until the ingredients are incorporated, but do not over-beat. Using a rubber spatula, scrape down the batter in the bowl, making sure the ingredients are well blended.

Divide the batter among the prepared tins and bake for 25–30 minutes or until a skewer inserted in the centre of the cake comes out clean. Let the layers cool in the tins for 1 hour. Remove from the tins and cool completely on a wire rack.

To make the cream filling, in a large bowl, whip the double cream with the sugar and vanilla until stiff peaks form.

To make the stawberry filling, gently toss the strawberries with the sugar to evenly coat the fruit.

To assemble the cake, when the cake layers have cooled completely, spread one-third of the whipped cream filling over the bottom cake layer, followed by one-third of the strawberry filling. Repeat with the remaining layers.

MAKES ONE 3-LAYER 23-CM (9-IN) CAKE

Red Velvet Cake
with Creamy Vanilla Icing

*T*his is one of our most popular cakes at the bakery. Half of the customers love it because they haven't eaten it since their grandmother made it when they were children and the other half because they think the red colour is really neat. But everyone thinks it's delicious.

CAKE
450 g (1 lb) superfine plain flour
175 g (6 oz) unsalted butter,
    softened
285 g (10 oz) sugar
3 eggs, at room temperature
90 ml (3 fl oz) red food colouring
3 tablespoons cocoa powder
1 ½ teaspoons vanilla extract

1 ½ teaspoons salt
350 ml (12 fl oz) buttermilk
1 ½ teaspoons cider vinegar
1 ½ teaspoons bicarbonate of soda

ICING
1 recipe Creamy Vanilla Icing
    (page 126)

Preheat the oven to Gas Mark 4/180°C/fan oven 160°C.

Grease and lightly flour three 23 x 5-cm (9 x 2-in) round cake tins, then base-line with greaseproof paper.

To make the cake, in a small bowl, sift the flour and set aside. In a large bowl, using the medium speed of an electric mixer, cream the butter and sugar for about 5 minutes until very light and fluffy. Add the eggs, one at a time, beating well after each addition.

In a small bowl, whisk together the red food colouring, cocoa and vanilla. Add to the batter and beat well.

In a measuring jug, stir the salt into the buttermilk. Add to the batter in three parts, alternating with the flour. With each addition, beat until the ingredients are incorporated, but do not over-beat.

In a small bowl, stir together the cider vinegar and bicarbonate of soda. Add to the batter and mix well. Using a rubber spatula, scrape down the batter in the bowl, making sure the ingredients are well blended and the batter is smooth.

Divide the batter among the prepared tins. Bake for 30–40 minutes or until a skewer inserted in the centre of the cake comes out clean. Let the layers cool in the tins for 1 hour. Remove from the tins and cool completely on a wire rack.

When the cake has cooled, spread the icing between the layers, then ice the top and sides of the cake with Creamy Vanilla Icing.

MAKES ONE 3-LAYER 23-CM (9-IN) CAKE

Magnolia's
Vanilla Cupcakes

*E*veryone is always asking us which is the most popular cupcake at the bakery. Most people are surprised that it is what we call the vanilla vanilla – the vanilla cupcake with the vanilla icing (and the most popular colour for the icing is pink).

CUPCAKES
185 g (6½ oz) self-raising flour
160 g (5½ oz) plain flour
225 g (8 oz) unsalted butter,
    softened
400 g (14 oz) sugar
4 eggs, at room temperature

250 ml (9 fl oz) milk
1 teaspoon vanilla extract

ICING
Vanilla Buttercream (page 117) or
    Chocolate Buttercream (page 122)

Preheat the oven to Gas Mark 4/180°C/fan oven 160°C.

Line two 12-hole muffin tins with cupcake paper cases.

In a small bowl, combine the flours. Set aside.

In a large bowl, using the medium speed of an electric mixer, cream the butter until smooth. Add the sugar gradually and beat for about 3 minutes until fluffy. Add the eggs, one at a time, beating well after each addition. Add the dry ingredients in three parts, alternating with the milk and vanilla. With each addition, beat until the ingredients are incorporated but do not over-beat. Using a rubber spatula, scrape down the batter in the bowl to make sure the ingredients are well blended. Carefully spoon the batter into the cupcake cases, filling them about three-quarters full. Bake for 20–25 minutes or until a skewer inserted into the centre of the cupcake comes out clean.

Cool the cupcakes in the tins for 15 minutes. Remove from the tins and cool completely on a wire rack before icing. At the bakery we ice the cupcakes with either Vanilla Buttercream or Chocolate Buttercream.

MAKES ABOUT 24 CUPCAKES
(DEPENDING ON THE SIZE OF YOUR CUPCAKE CASES AND MUFFIN TINS)

Note: If you would like to make a layer cake instead of cupcakes, divide the batter between two 23-cm (9-in) round cake tins and bake the layers for 30–40 minutes.

Devil's Food Cake with
Seven-minute Icing and Coconut

This is the same recipe we've made in my family for every birthday since the beginning of time and the same cake we serve at the bakery – but a different icing and the coconut decoration give it a whole new taste.

CAKE
375 g (13 oz) plain flour
1 ½ teaspoons baking powder
1 ½ teaspoons bicarbonate of soda
¾ teaspoon salt
175 g (6 oz) unsalted butter,
    softened
250 g (9 oz) light brown sugar
3 eggs, separated, at room
    temperature (see first Note)

250 g (9 oz) plain chocolate, melted
    (see second Note)
475 ml (17 fl oz) milk
1 ½ teaspoons vanilla extract

ICING
One recipe Seven-minute Icing
    (page 125)

DECORATION
Desiccated coconut

Notes:

It is best to separate the eggs when cold and then allow them to come to room temperature before proceeding with the recipe.

To melt the chocolate, place it in a double boiler over simmering water on a low heat for 5–10 minutes. Or use a heatproof bowl set over a saucepan of simmering water (but do not allow the base of the bowl to touch the water). Stir occasionally until completely smooth. Remove from the heat and allow to cool for 5–10 minutes to lukewarm.

Preheat the oven to Gas Mark 4/180°C/fan oven 160°C.
    Grease and lightly flour three 23 x 5-cm (9 x 2-in) round cake tins, then base-line with greaseproof paper.

In a small bowl, sift together the flour, baking powder, bicarbonate of soda and salt. Set aside.

In a large bowl, using the medium speed of an electric mixer, cream the butter until smooth. Add the sugar and beat for about 3 minutes until fluffy.

In a separate small bowl, beat the egg yolks for about 2 minutes until thick and lemon-coloured. Add the beaten yolks to the butter mixture and beat well. Add the chocolate, mixing until well incorporated. Add the dry ingredients in three parts, alternating with the milk and vanilla. With each addition, beat until the ingredients are incorporated, but do not over-beat. Using a rubber spatula, scrape down the batter in the bowl, making sure the ingredients are well blended and the batter is smooth.

In a separate small bowl, beat the egg whites using the high speed of an electric mixer until soft peaks form. Gently fold into the batter. Divide the batter among the prepared tins and bake for 30–35 minutes or until a skewer inserted in the centre of the cake comes out clean.

Let the layers cool in the tins for 1 hour. Remove from the tins and allow to cool completely on a wire rack.

When the cake has cooled, ice between the layers, then ice the top and sides of the cake with Seven-minute Icing. Sprinkle the top of the cake generously with the coconut.

MAKES ONE 3-LAYER 23-CM (9-IN) CAKE

Banana Cake with White Chocolate Cream Cheese Icing

This recipe came about because I wanted to make a banana cake using butter instead of the traditional oil as the vegetable fat. The result is a cake with a very different and quite lovely texture and it's perfectly complemented by the white chocolate icing.

CAKE

400 g (14 oz) superfine plain flour
1 teaspoon bicarbonate of soda
¾ teaspoon salt
½ teaspoon baking powder
225 g (8 oz) unsalted butter, softened
400 g (14 oz) sugar
3 eggs, at room temperature
375 g (13 oz) mashed very ripe
    bananas

90 ml (3 fl oz) buttermilk
1 ½ teaspoons vanilla extract

ICING

1 recipe White Chocolate Cream
    Cheese Icing (page 127)

DECORATION

100 g (3 ½ oz) walnuts, chopped, or
    walnut halves

Preheat the oven to Gas Mark 3/160°C/fan oven 140°C.

Grease and lightly flour two 23 x 5-cm (9 x 2-in) round cake tins, then base-line with greaseproof paper.

To make the cake, in a small bowl, sift together the flour, bicarbonate of soda, salt and baking powder. Set aside.

In a large bowl, using the medium speed of an electric mixer, cream the butter until smooth. Add the sugar gradually and beat for about 3 minutes until fluffy. Add the eggs, one at a time, beating well after each addition. Add the bananas. Add half of the dry ingredients, mixing until well incorporated, then add the buttermilk and vanilla and then the second half of the dry ingredients, mixing well. Divide the batter between the prepared tins. Bake for 40–50 minutes or until a skewer inserted in the centre of the cake comes out clean.

Let the layers cool in the tins for 1 hour. Remove from the tins and allow to cool completely on a wire rack.

When the cake has cooled, ice between the layers with White Chocolate Cream Cheese Icing, then ice the top and sides of the cake. Decorate with the walnuts as wished.

MAKES ONE 2-LAYER 23-CM (9-IN) CAKE

Caramel Pecan Layer Cake

A light, moist vanilla cake iced with creamy caramel icing and generous amounts of toasted pecan nuts. It is a wonderful birthday cake alternative if you want to serve something different from the traditional yellow or chocolate cake.

CAKE
185 g (6½ oz) self-raising flour
160 g (5½ oz) plain flour
225 g (8 oz) unsalted butter, softened
400 g (14 oz) sugar
4 eggs, at room temperature
250 ml (9 fl oz) milk
1 teaspoon vanilla extract

ICING
1 recipe Caramel Icing (page 119)

DECORATION
175 g (6 oz) toasted pecan nuts, coarsely chopped (see Note)

Note: To toast the pecan nuts, place them on a baking tray in a Gas Mark 4/180°C/fan oven 160°C oven for 15 minutes or until lightly browned and fragrant.

Preheat the oven to Gas Mark 4/180°C/fan oven 160°C.

Grease and lightly flour three 23 x 5-cm (9 x 2-in) round cake tins, then base-line with greaseproof paper.

To make the cake, in a small bowl, combine the flours and set aside. In a large bowl, using the medium speed of an electric mixer, cream the butter until smooth. Add the sugar gradually and beat for about 3 minutes until fluffy. Add the eggs, one at a time, beating well after each addition. Add the dry ingredients in three parts, alternating with the milk and vanilla. With each addition, beat until the ingredients are incorporated, but do not over-beat. Using a rubber spatula, scrape down the batter in the bowl, making sure the ingredients are well blended.

Divide the batter among the prepared tins and bake for 25–30 minutes or until a skewer inserted in the centre of the cake comes out clean. Let the layers cool in the tins for 1 hour. Remove the layers from the tins and cool completely on a wire rack.

When the layers have cooled completely, ice the cake by filling between the layers first with the Caramel Icing and then sprinkling with one-third of the pecans on each layer. Then ice the top and sides of the cake and sprinkle the top with the remaining pecans.

MAKES ONE 3-LAYER 23-CM (9-IN) CAKE

Magnolia's
Chocolate Cupcakes

Made from the same batter as our popular Chocolate Buttermilk Cake, this not too rich and not too chocolatey cupcake goes equally well with the vanilla or chocolate buttercream icing.

CUPCAKES
250 g (9 oz) plain flour
1 teaspoon bicarbonate of soda
225 g (8 oz) unsalted butter, softened
200 g (7 oz) granulated sugar
225 g (8 oz) light brown sugar
4 eggs, at room temperature

175 g (6 oz) plain chocolate, melted (see Note)
250 ml (9 fl oz) buttermilk
1 teaspoon vanilla extract

ICING
Vanilla Buttercream (page 117) or
    Chocolate Buttercream (page 122)

Note: To melt the chocolate, place in a double boiler over simmering water on a low heat for 5–10 minutes. Or use a heatproof bowl set over a saucepan of simmering water (but do not allow the base of the bowl to touch the water). Stir occasionally until completely smooth. Remove from the heat and let cool for 5–10 minutes until lukewarm.

Preheat the oven to Gas Mark 4/180°C/fan oven 160°C.

Line two 12-hole muffin tins with cupcake paper cases. Set aside.

In a small bowl, sift together the flour and bicarbonate of soda. Set aside.

In a large bowl, using the medium speed of an electric mixer, cream the butter until smooth. Add the sugars and beat for about 3 minutes until fluffy. Add the eggs, one at a time, beating well after each addition. Add the chocolate, mixing until well incorporated. Add the dry ingredients in three parts, alternating with the buttermilk and vanilla. With each addition, beat until the ingredients are incorporated, but do not over-beat. Using a rubber spatula, scrape down the batter in the bowl to make sure the ingredients are well blended and the batter is smooth. Carefully spoon the batter into the cupcake cases, filling them about three-quarters full. Bake for 20–25 minutes, or until a skewer inserted in the centre of the cupcake comes out clean.

Cool the cupcakes in the tins for 15 minutes. Remove from the tins and cool completely on a wire rack before icing. At the bakery we ice the cupcakes with either Vanilla Buttercream or Chocolate Buttercream.

MAKES ABOUT 24 CUPCAKES

(DEPENDING ON THE SIZE OF YOUR CUPCAKE PAPER CASES AND MUFFIN TINS)

Note: If you would like to make a layer cake instead of cupcakes, divide the batter between two 23-cm (9-in) round cake tins and bake for 30–40 minutes.

Carrot Cake

We don't make carrot cake at the bakery (I can just hear the Hummingbird cake fans screaming), but this is the cake I make most often at home. We love it.

CAKE
250 g (9 oz) plain flour
1 teaspoon baking powder
1 teaspoon cinnamon
½ teaspoon salt
250 ml (9 fl oz) vegetable oil
　　(preferably rapeseed)
350 g (12 oz) sugar
3 eggs, at room temperature
1½ teaspoons vanilla extract
225 g (8 oz) carrots, grated
225 g (8 oz) canned crushed
　　pineapple in its own juice

115 g (4 oz) toasted pecan nuts,
　　coarsely chopped (see Note)
70 g (2½ oz) desiccated coconut

ICING
1 recipe Cream Cheese Icing
　　(page 118)

DECORATION
Toasted pecan nuts, coarsely chopped
　　(see Note)

Note: To toast the pecan nuts, place them on a baking tray in a Gas Mark 4/180°C/ fan oven 160°C oven for 15 minutes or until lightly browned and fragrant.

Preheat the oven to Gas Mark 3/160°C/fan oven 140°C.

Grease and lightly flour two 23 x 5-cm (9 x 2-in) round cake tins, then base-line with greaseproof paper.

In a small bowl, sift together the flour, baking powder, cinnamon and salt. Set aside.

In a large bowl, using the medium speed of an electric mixer, beat together the oil and sugar. Add the eggs, one at a time, and beat for about 2 minutes until light and thick. Add the vanilla and beat well. Gradually add the dry ingredients, beating until well incorporated. Stir in the carrots, pineapple and its juice, pecans and coconut.

Divide the batter between the prepared tins and bake for 40–50 minutes, or until a skewer inserted in the centre of the cake comes out clean. Allow the layers to cool in the tins for 1 hour. Remove from the tins and cool completely on a wire rack.

When the cake has cooled, ice between the layers, then ice the top and sides of the cake with Cream Cheese Icing. Decorate with the toasted pecans if wished.

MAKES ONE 2-LAYER 23-CM (9-IN) CAKE

Devil's Food Cupcakes with Caramel Icing

I love this particular chocolate cake, so I thought a second recipe seemed like a really good idea. This recipe is very different from the rich chocolate cake recipe – more chocolatey and extremely light in texture. These cupcakes are great with the caramel icing, but I wouldn't hesitate to try them with other icings as well.

CUPCAKES
275 g (9½ oz) superfine plain flour
100 g (3½ oz) cocoa powder
1½ teaspoons bicarbonate of soda
½ teaspoon salt
175 g (6 oz) unsalted butter, softened
325 g (11½ oz) soft light brown sugar

100 g (3½ oz) granulated sugar
3 eggs, at room temperature
350 ml (12 fl oz) buttermilk
2 teaspoons vanilla extract

ICING
1 recipe Caramel Icing (page 119)

Preheat the oven to Gas Mark 4/180°C/fan oven 160°C.

Line three 12-hole muffin tins with cupcake paper cases. Set aside.

In a small bowl, sift the flour, cocoa, bicarbonate of soda and salt. Set aside.

In a large bowl, using the medium speed of an electric mixer, cream the butter until smooth. Add the sugars and beat for about 3 minutes until fluffy. Add the eggs, one at a time, beating well after each addition. Add the dry ingredients in three parts, alternating with the buttermilk and vanilla. With each addition, beat until the ingredients are incorporated, but do not over-beat. Using a rubber spatula, scrape down the batter in the bowl, making sure the ingredients are well blended. Carefully spoon the batter into the cupcake cases, filling them about three-quarters full. Bake for 25–30 minutes or until a skewer inserted in the centre of the cupcake comes out clean.

Cool the cupcakes in the tins for 15 minutes. Remove from the tins and cool completely on a wire rack before icing with Caramel Icing.

MAKES ABOUT 30 CUPCAKES
(DEPENDING ON THE SIZE OF YOUR CUPCAKE PAPER CASES AND MUFFIN TINS)

Apple Cake with Butterscotch Cream Cheese Icing

A fluffy, golden cake with chunks of apples and a sweet, creamy icing. If you're not a butterscotch fan, this cake is also good iced with vanilla buttercream.

CAKE
375 g (13 oz) plain flour
2 teaspoons baking powder
½ teaspoon salt
225 g (8 oz) unsalted butter, softened
400 g (14 oz) sugar
5 eggs, at room temperature
250 ml (9 fl oz) milk

1 ½ teaspoons vanilla extract
375 g (13 oz) peeled crisp tart apples, coarsely chopped

ICING
1 recipe Butterscotch Cream Cheese Icing (page 123)

Preheat the oven to Gas Mark 3/160°C/fan oven 140°C.

Grease and lightly flour two 23-cm (9-in) round cake tins, then base-line with greaseproof paper.

In a small bowl, sift together the flour, baking powder and salt. Set aside. In a large bowl, using the medium speed of an electric mixer, cream the butter until smooth. Add the sugar gradually and beat for about 3 minutes until fluffy. Add the eggs, one at a time, beating well after each addition. Add the dry ingredients in three parts, alternating with the milk and vanilla. With each addition, beat until the ingredients are incorporated, but do not over-beat. Using a rubber spatula, scrape down the batter in the bowl, making sure the ingredients are well blended. Stir in the apples.

Divide the batter between the prepared tins. Bake for 40–50 minutes or until a skewer inserted in the centre of the cake comes out clean.

Let the layers cool in the tins for 1 hour. Remove from the tins and allow to cool completely on a wire rack. When the cake has cooled, ice between the layers, then ice the top and sides of the cake with Butterscotch Cream Cheese Icing.

MAKES ONE 2-LAYER 23-CM (9-IN) CAKE

Ice Creams and Chilled Desserts

White Chocolate
Peanut Brittle Ice Cream

This has been our most popular ice cream flavour both at the bakery and in grocery stores since we launched our ice cream line in 2001. The peanut brittle complements the brown-sugar-based custard perfectly.

3 egg yolks, at room temperature
475 ml (17 fl oz) single cream
150 g (5 oz) soft light brown sugar
3 tablespoons golden syrup
1 tablespoon vanilla extract

185 g (6½ oz) peanut brittle bars, coarsely chopped
85 g (3 oz) white chocolate (preferably Lindt), coarsely chopped

In a medium-sized bowl, using an electric mixer or a whisk, beat the egg yolks for 2–3 minutes until creamy. Set aside.

In a medium saucepan, combine the single cream, sugar and syrup and cook over a medium heat, stirring constantly, until the sugar is completely dissolved. Remove from the heat and add 125 ml (4 fl oz) of the cream mixture to the egg yolks, stirring to warm the egg yolks. Return the entire mixture to the pan and continue to cook, stirring continuously for about 10 minutes until it coats the back of the spoon. Remove from the heat and place the pan in a bowl of cold water. When the custard has cooled to room temperature, stir in the vanilla. Cover and refrigerate until completely chilled, preferably overnight.

Pour into an ice cream machine and freeze for about 20 minutes until partially set. Stir in the chopped peanut bars and white chocolate and continue freezing until firm, following the manufacturer's instructions.

MAKES ABOUT 1 LITRE (1¾ PINTS)

Old-fashioned
Chocolate Chip Ice Cream

I've been making this ice cream since I was a child and we got our first ice cream machine. It's always been both my dad and my brother's favourite flavour.

6 egg yolks, at room temperature
125 g (4½ oz) sugar
475 ml (17 fl oz) single cream
250 ml (9 fl oz) double cream

1 tablespoon vanilla extract
175 g (6 oz) miniature plain chocolate chips

In a medium-sized bowl, using an electric mixer or a whisk, beat the egg yolks for 2–3 minutes until creamy. Add the sugar and beat until incorporated. Set aside.

In a double boiler over simmering water (or a heatproof bowl set over a saucepan of simmering water), heat the single cream until scalded. Add 125 ml (4 fl oz) of the single cream to the egg mixture, stirring to warm the egg yolks. Return the entire mixture to the double boiler and continue to cook, stirring constantly for about 10 minutes until the mixture coats the back of a spoon. Remove from the heat and place the pan in a bowl of cold water. When the custard has cooled to room temperature, stir in the double cream and vanilla. Cover and refrigerate until completely chilled, preferably overnight.

Pour into an ice cream machine and freeze for about 20 minutes until partially set. Stir in the chocolate chips and continue freezing until firm, following the manufacturer's instructions.

MAKES ABOUT 1 LITRE (1¾ PINTS)

Vanilla Layer Creme Cookie Ice Cream

For vanilla lovers like myself, this is like the well-known 'cookies and cream' or 'Oreo' ice creams, but it is made with vanilla cookies instead of chocolate. It's another big favourite at the bakery.

6 egg yolks, at room temperature
125 g (4½ oz) sugar
475 ml (17 fl oz) single cream
250 ml (9 fl oz) double cream

1 tablespoon vanilla extract
12 vanilla layer cookies, broken into
    quarters

In a medium-sized bowl, using an electric mixer or a whisk, beat the egg yolks for 2–3 minutes until creamy. Add the sugar and beat until incorporated. Set aside.

In a double boiler over simmering water (or heatproof bowl set over a saucepan of simmering water), heat the single cream until scalded. Add 125 ml (4 fl oz) of the single cream to the egg mixture, stirring to warm the egg yolks. Return the entire mixture to the double boiler and continue to cook, stirring continuously for about 10 minutes until the mixture coats the back of a spoon. Remove from the heat and place the pan in a bowl of cold water. When the custard has cooled to room temperature, stir in the cream and vanilla. Cover and refrigerate until completely chilled, preferably overnight.

Pour into an ice cream machine and freeze for about 20 minutes until partially set. Stir in the broken cookie pieces and continue freezing until firm, following the manufacturer's instructions.

MAKES ABOUT 1 LITRE (1¾ PINTS)

Chilled Caramel Toffee Pecan Pie

A brown sugar shortbread base, a creamy caramel filling and a topping of Heath bars and toasted pecan nuts – I don't think one could want much more in a chilled dessert.

Base
85 g (3 oz) plain flour
75 g (2¾ oz) soft light brown sugar
75 g (2¾ oz) toasted pecan nuts, chopped (see Note)
85 g (3 oz) unsalted butter, softened and cut into small pieces

Filling
350 g (12 oz) vanilla caramels
3 tablespoons double cream

350 g (12 oz) cream cheese, softened
175 ml (6 fl oz) double cream

Decoration
55 g (2 oz) Heath bars or chocolate-covered toffee pieces, chopped
75 g (2¾ oz) toasted pecan nuts, chopped (see Note)

Note: To toast the pecan nuts, place them on a baking tray in an oven at Gas Mark 4/180°C/fan oven 160°C for 15 minutes or until lightly browned and fragrant.

Preheat the oven to Gas Mark 3/160°C/fan oven 140°C.

To make the base, in a medium-sized bowl, combine the flour, sugar and pecans. Rub in the butter until the mixture resembles coarse crumbs. Press into the base of a 23-cm (9-in) pie dish.

Bake the base for 12–15 minutes or until lightly golden. Remove from the oven and allow to cool for about 45 minutes to reach room temperature.

To make the filling, in a medium-sized saucepan over a low heat, melt the caramels with the 3 tablespoons of cream, stirring occasionally until smooth. Remove from the heat and allow to cool for about 30 minutes to reach room temperature.

In a large bowl, using the medium speed of an electric mixer, beat the cream cheese until smooth. Add the cooled caramel and beat well.

In a separate bowl, beat the 175 ml (6 fl oz) of double cream until stiff peaks form. Gently fold the whipped cream into the cream cheese mixture until well blended and no streaks of cream remain. Spoon the filling into the cooled base.

To decorate, sprinkle the Heath pieces and pecans around the edge of the pie. Cover with cling film and chill overnight in the refrigerator before serving.

MAKES ONE 23-CM (9-IN) PIE

Heavenly Hash
Ice Cream Pie

Heavenly Hash was one of my favourite flavours of ice cream when I was growing up. It's difficult to find these days, so I decided to put the ingredients together in an ice cream pie and give up my supermarket search. You can use chocolate or vanilla ice cream in this recipe (or a layer of each) – both versions are great.

Base

115 g (4 oz) unsalted butter, melted
175 g (6 oz) chocolate cookie crumbs

Marshmallow Sauce

225 g (8 oz) miniature marshmallows
5 tablespoons double cream

Filling

1 litre (1 ¾ pints) chocolate ice cream
100 g (3 ½ oz) toasted almonds, coarsely chopped (see Note)
40 g (1 ½ oz) miniature plain chocolate chips

Note: To toast the almonds, place them on a baking tray in an oven at Gas Mark 4/180°C/fan oven 160°C for 15 minutes or until lightly browned and fragrant.

To make the base, in a medium-sized bowl, combine the butter and cookie crumbs. Press firmly into a lightly buttered 23-cm (9-in) pie dish. Cover tightly with cling film and place in the freezer for 1 hour.

To make the marshmallow sauce, in the top of a double boiler over barely simmering water (or use a heatproof bowl set over a saucepan of barely simmering water), combine the marshmallows with the cream. Stir for 3–5 minutes until the marshmallows are completely melted and the sauce is smooth. Remove from the heat and transfer the sauce to a glass measuring jug. Allow to cool for 20 minutes.

Meanwhile, transfer the ice cream from the freezer to a covered plastic storage tub and place in the refrigerator to soften for 20 minutes.

Remove the base from the freezer and the ice cream from the refrigerator. Using a wooden spoon, stir the ice cream until creamy and of good spreading consistency. Spread half of the ice cream over the prepared base. (I recommend using a small offset icing spatula if you have one.) Pour the marshmallow sauce evenly over the ice cream and sprinkle with half of the almonds. Cover tightly with cling film and place in the freezer for 15 minutes to set. (Place the remaining ice cream in the freezer as well so that it doesn't get too soft.)

Remove the pie and ice cream from the freezer and carefully spread the remaining ice cream evenly over the top layer. To decorate, sprinkle the remaining almonds and the chocolate chips around the edge of the pie. Cover tightly with cling film and then kitchen foil and freeze for at least 4 hours or overnight until the pie is firm.

Allow the pie to soften slightly for about 10 minutes at room temperature before slicing and serving.

MAKES ONE 23-CM (9-IN) PIE

Cherry Jamboree

We started making this a few years ago when a staff member remarked that her grandmother made a dessert like our cream cheese chocolate pudding squares but with cherry pie filling. It turned out to be even more popular, so we're still making it.

BASE
125 g (4½ oz) plain flour
55 g (2 oz) toasted pecan nuts, chopped (see Note)
75 g (2¾ oz) unsalted butter, melted

CREAM CHEESE FILLING
225 g (8 oz) cream cheese, softened
125 g (4½ oz) icing sugar, sifted
250 ml (9 fl oz) double cream

TOPPING
600 g (1 lb 5 oz) canned cherry pie filling

DECORATION
Sweet Vanilla Whipped Cream (page 121)
Toasted pecan nut halves (see Note)

Note: To toast the pecan nuts, place them on a baking tray in an oven at Gas Mark 4/180°C/ fan oven 160°C for 15 minutes or until lightly browned and fragrant.

Preheat the oven to Gas Mark 5/190°C/fan oven 170°C.

To make the base, in a small bowl, combine the flour, pecans and butter. Press firmly into the base of an ungreased 20 x 20-cm (8 x 8-in) glass baking dish. Bake for 15 minutes. Remove from the oven and allow to cool on a wire rack.

To make the filling, in a large bowl, using the low speed of an electric mixer, beat the cream cheese for about 2 minutes until smooth. Add the sugar and beat well. In a separate small bowl, beat the double cream until stiff peaks form. Gently fold the cream into the cream cheese mixture and spread evenly over the cooled base using a rubber spatula. Spread the cherry pie filling on top. Cover with cling film and chill for at least 2 hours or overnight. Cut into squares and serve with a dollop of cream and the pecan halves.

MAKES NINE 6-CM (2½-IN) SQUARES

Magnolia's Famous Banana Pudding

I started making this pudding when I was in my early twenties and cooking at a Tex-Mex restaurant and bar. Customers loved it, so when we opened the bakery many years later, it seemed like a great idea to serve it there. It remains the second most popular dessert (after the cupcakes) at the bakery.

400 g (14 oz) canned condensed milk
350 ml (12 fl oz) ice cold water
100 g (3½ oz) instant vanilla pudding mix or instant custard mix

750 ml (1¼ pints) double cream
350 g (12 oz) Nabisco Nilla Wafers or other soft vanilla cookies, or sponge fingers
900 g (2 lb) ripe bananas, sliced

In a small bowl, using the medium speed of an electric mixer, beat together the condensed milk and water for about 1 minute until well combined. Add the pudding mix and beat well for about a further 2 minutes. Cover and refrigerate for 3–4 hours or overnight before continuing. It is very important to allow the proper amount of time for the pudding mixture to set.

In a large bowl, using the medium speed of an electric mixer, whip the double cream until stiff peaks form. Gently fold the pudding mixture into the whipped cream until well blended and no streaks of pudding remain.

To assemble the dessert, select a large, wide bowl (preferably glass) with a 4–5 litre (7–9 pint) capacity. Cover the base of the bowl with one-third of the cookies, overlapping if necessary, then layer with one-third of the bananas and one-third of the pudding. Repeat the layering twice more, decorating with additional cookie or cookie crumbs on the top layer of the pudding. Cover tightly with cling film and allow to chill in the refrigerator for 4 hours – or up to 8 hours, but no longer! – before serving.

SERVES 12–15

Lemon Pudding with Raspberries and Ginger Nut Cookies

Magnolia day manager Margaret Hathaway came up with this delightful spring-time dessert that is based on our banana pudding.

8 egg yolks, at room temperature
400 g (14 oz) sugar
65 g (2¼ oz) cornflour
750 ml (1¼ pints) warm water
115 g (4 oz) unsalted butter, melted
    and cooled to room temperature

350 ml (12 fl oz) fresh lemon juice
1 teaspoon grated lemon zest
750 ml (1¼ pints) double cream
350 g (12 oz) ginger nut cookies
250 g (9 oz) fresh raspberries

In a medium-sized bowl, using an electric mixer or a whisk, beat the egg yolks for 2–3 minutes until creamy. Set aside.

In a large saucepan, combine the sugar and cornflour. Gradually add the water and cook over a medium heat, stirring continuously for about 5 minutes until the mixture thickens. Remove from the heat and add 475 ml (17 fl oz) of the hot mixture to the egg yolks, stirring to warm the egg yolks. Return the entire mixture to the pan and heat for a further 1 minute.

Remove from the heat and stir in the butter, lemon juice and lemon zest. Transfer to a medium-sized bowl and cool for about 1 hour to room temperature.

In a large bowl, using the medium speed of an electric mixer, whip the cream until stiff peaks form. Gently fold the pudding mixture into the whipped cream until well blended and no streaks of pudding remain.

To assemble the dessert, select a large, wide bowl (preferably glass) with a 4–5 litre (7–9 pint) capacity. Arrange one-third of the ginger nut cookies to cover the base of the bowl, overlapping if necessary, then one-third of the pudding. Repeat the layering twice more. Decorate the top layer with raspberries. Cover tightly with cling film and allow to chill in the refrigerator for 4 hours – or up to 8 hours, but no longer! – before serving.

SERVES 12–15

Icings and Sauces

Vanilla Buttercream

The vanilla buttercream we use at the bakery is technically not a buttercream but actually an old-fashioned icing sugar and butter icing. Make sure you beat the icing for the amount of time called for in the recipe to achieve the desired creamy texture.

225 g (8 oz) unsalted butter, softened
75g–1 kg (1 lb 10 oz–2 lb 4 oz) sifted
   icing sugar

125 ml (4 fl oz) milk
2 teaspoons vanilla extract

Place the butter in a large mixing bowl. Add 500 g (1 lb 2 oz) of the sugar and then the milk and vanilla. Using the medium speed of an electric mixer, beat for 3–5 minutes until smooth and creamy. Gradually add the remaining sugar, 125 g (4½ oz) at a time, beating well after each addition for about 2 minutes, until the icing is thick enough to be of good spreading consistency. You may not need to add all of the sugar. If wished, add a few drops of food colouring and mix thoroughly. (Use and store the icing at room temperature because the icing will set if chilled.) The icing can be stored in an airtight container for up to 3 days.

MAKES ENOUGH FOR ONE 2-LAYER 23-CM (9-IN) CAKE OR 24 CUPCAKES

Note: If you are icing a 3-layer cake, use the following recipe proportions:

350 g (12 oz) unsalted butter
1–1.25 kg (2 lb 4 oz–2 lb 12 oz)
   sifted icing sugar

175 ml (6 fl oz) milk
1 tablespoon vanilla extract

Cream Cheese Icing

Cream cheese icing is probably my favourite icing and I haven't yet found anyone who doesn't like it. It's the traditional icing for carrot cake, but is delicious with many other desserts as well.

450 g (1 lb) cream cheese, softened
    and cut into small pieces
85 g (3 oz) unsalted butter, softened
    and cut into small pieces

1 ½ teaspoons vanilla extract
500 g (1 lb 2 oz) sifted icing sugar

In a large bowl, using the medium speed of an electric mixer, beat the cream cheese and butter for about 3 minutes until smooth. Add the vanilla and beat well. Gradually add the sugar, 100 g (3½ oz) at a time, beating continuously until smooth and creamy. Cover and refrigerate the icing for 2–3 hours, but no longer, to thicken before using.

MAKES ENOUGH FOR ONE 2- OR 3-LAYER 23-CM (9-IN) CAKE

Caramel Icing

I love anything with caramel and I always wanted to make an easy caramel icing that didn't involve a sugar thermometer. Here it is. (This icing tastes better if made the day before the cake because the brown sugar gives the icing a slightly grainy texture that improves if allowed to set overnight.)

450 g (1 lb) unsalted butter,
    softened
500 g (1 lb 2 oz) sifted icing sugar
325 g (11 ½ oz) soft light brown sugar

125 ml (4 fl oz) milk
2 tablespoons golden syrup
2 teaspoons vanilla extract

In a large bowl, using the medium speed of an electric mixer, cream the butter until smooth. Add the sugars and beat on a low speed for 2 minutes. Add the milk, syrup and vanilla and beat for 3–5 minutes until smooth and creamy. Use immediately or store, covered, at room temperature for up to 2 days.

MAKES ENOUGH FOR ONE 3-LAYER 23-CM (9-IN) CAKE OR 36 CUPCAKES

White Chocolate
Buttercream

I'm one of those people who prefers white chocolate to chocolate and the visual contrast of the white icing with a chocolate cake is wonderful.

350 g (12 oz) unsalted butter, softened
90 ml (3 fl oz) milk
250 g (9 oz) white chocolate, melted and cooled to lukewarm (see Note)

1 teaspoon vanilla extract
300 g (10½ oz) sifted icing sugar

Note: To melt the chocolate, place it in a double boiler over simmering water on a low heat for about 5–10 minutes. Or set a heatproof bowl over a saucepan of simmering water (but do not allow the base of the bowl to touch the water). Stir occasionally until completely smooth. Remove from the heat and let cool for 5–10 minutes until lukewarm.

In a large bowl, using the medium speed of an electric mixer, beat the butter for about 3 minutes until creamy. Add the milk carefully and beat until smooth. Add the melted chocolate and beat well for about 2 minutes. Add the vanilla and beat for 3 minutes. Gradually add the sugar and beat on a low speed until creamy and of the desired consistency.

MAKES ENOUGH FOR ONE 2-LAYER 23-CM (9-IN) CAKE OR 24 CUPCAKES

Note: If you are icing a 3-layer cake, use the following recipe proportions:

450 g (1 lb) unsalted butter
125 ml (4 fl oz) milk
350 g (12 oz) white chocolate

1½ teaspoons vanilla extract
400 g (14 oz) sifted icing sugar

Sweet Vanilla Whipped Cream

I believe that no pie is complete without a large dollop of whipped cream to accompany it. Since I suggest it so often in my recipes, I thought I should include my version of not-too-sweet whipped cream.

475 ml (17 fl oz) double cream
2 teaspoons sugar

2 teaspoons vanilla extract

Place all the ingredients in a medium-sized bowl and whip with an electric mixer or a whisk until soft peaks form. Serve immediately with your favourite dessert, or cover tightly with cling film and refrigerate for up to 4 hours.

Chocolate Buttercream

The key to achieving the same creamy texture that we do at the bakery is in beating the icing at the proper speeds for the proper amount of time. If beaten at too high a speed, the icing incorporates a lot of air and becomes fluffy rather than creamy.

350 g (12 oz) unsalted butter, softened
2 tablespoons milk

250 g (9 oz) plain chocolate, melted and cooled to lukewarm (see Note)
1 teaspoon vanilla extract
225 g (8 oz) sifted icing sugar

Note: To melt the chocolate, place it in a double boiler over simmering water on a low heat for about 5–10 minutes. Or set a heatproof bowl over a saucepan of simmering water (but do not allow the base of the bowl to touch the water). Stir occasionally until completely smooth. Remove from the heat and let cool for 5–10 minutes until lukewarm.

In a large bowl, using the medium speed of an electric mixer, beat the butter for about 3 minutes until creamy. Add the milk carefully and beat until smooth. Add the melted chocolate and beat well for about 2 minutes. Add the vanilla and beat for 3 minutes. Gradually add the sugar and beat on a low speed until creamy and of the desired consistency.

MAKES ENOUGH FOR ONE 2-LAYER 23-CM (9-IN) CAKE OR 24 CUPCAKES

Note: If you are icing a 3-layer cake, use the following recipe proportions:

450 g (1 lb) unsalted butter
3 tablespoons milk
350 g (12 oz) plain chocolate

1 ½ teaspoons vanilla extract
300 g (10½ oz) icing sugar

Butterscotch Cream Cheese Icing

This not-so-sweet icing combines a deep butterscotch flavour with the tanginess of the cream cheese. It goes just wonderfully with the apple layer cake.

450 g (1 lb) cream cheese, softened
85 g (3 oz) unsalted butter, softened

225 g (8 oz) soft light brown sugar
2 tablespoons golden syrup
1 teaspoon vanilla extract

In a large bowl, using the medium speed of an electric mixer, beat the cream cheese and butter for about 3 minutes until smooth. Add the sugar, syrup and vanilla and beat until smooth and creamy.

Cover and refrigerate the icing for 1 hour to thicken before using.

Makes enough for one 2- or 3-layer 23-cm (9-in) cake

Caramel Sauce

*C*aramel is not difficult to prepare, but it has to be done correctly. Pay attention as it nears the end of cooking because it can go from deep amber to burnt very, very quickly.

250 ml (9 fl oz) cold water
375 g (13 oz) sugar

475 ml (17 fl oz) double cream, at
room temperature

In a medium-sized saucepan, combine the water and sugar. Set over a medium-low heat, stirring occasionally, for about 3 minutes until the sugar dissolves, making sure no sugar is sticking to the sides of the pan. Increase the heat to high and boil without stirring for about 15 minutes until the syrup becomes a deep amber colour. To prevent the syrup becoming grainy, use a pastry brush dipped into cold water to brush down any sugar crystals sticking to the sides of the pan. Swirl the pan occasionally for even browning.

Once the syrup turns deep amber in colour, immediately remove from the heat. Slowly and carefully add the cream to the syrup (the mixture will bubble vigorously), whisking continuously until the cream is incorporated.

Return the pan to a medium-low heat and stir for about 1 minute until the sauce is smooth.

Remove from the heat and allow to come to room temperature before refrigerating. The caramel can be stored for up to 1 month in the refrigerator.

MAKES 800 ML (28 FL OZ)

Seven-minute Icing

This classic American marshmallow-like icing is a childhood favourite of many. It is a cooked icing but is relatively simple to make and can be used to ice a wide variety of cakes.

3 egg whites
450 g (1 lb) sugar
125 ml (4 fl oz) cold water

1 ½ tablespoons golden syrup
⅛ teaspoon salt
1 ½ teaspoons vanilla extract

Combine the egg whites, sugar, water, syrup and salt in the top of a double boiler and place over rapidly boiling water. (Or use a heatproof bowl over a saucepan of rapidly boiling water.) Using the high speed of an electric mixer, beat continuously for 6–8 minutes or until the icing stands up in soft peaks. Remove from the heat, add the vanilla and beat for about a further 1 minute or until the icing has the desired spreading consistency. Use immediately.

MAKES ENOUGH FOR ONE 2- OR 3-LAYER 23-CM (9-IN) CAKE

Creamy Vanilla Icing

*T*his silky smooth icing is made by beating together softened butter and sugar with a thick, sauce-like base. Make sure you follow the recipe directions exactly.

50 g (1 ¾ oz) plain flour
475 ml (17 fl oz) milk
450 g (1 lb) unsalted butter,
    softened

400 g (14 oz) sugar
2 teaspoons vanilla extract

In a medium-sized saucepan, whisk the flour into the milk until smooth. Place over a medium heat and, stirring continuously, cook for 10–15 minutes until the mixture becomes very thick and begins to bubble. Cover with greaseproof paper placed directly on the surface and allow to stand for about 30 minutes to cool to room temperature.

In a large bowl, using the medium-high speed of an electric mixer, beat the butter for about 3 minutes until smooth and creamy. Gradually add the sugar, beating continuously for about 3 minutes until fluffy. Add the vanilla and beat well.

Add the cooled milk mixture and continue to beat on the medium-high speed for 5 minutes until very smooth and noticeably whiter in colour. Cover and refrigerate for 15 minutes (no less and no longer – set a timer!). Use immediately.

MAKES ENOUGH FOR ONE 3-LAYER 23-CM (9-IN) CAKE

White Chocolate Cream Cheese Icing

What can I say – white chocolate and cream cheese together in a fabulous icing that's just perfect with the banana layer cake. (It's also really good on the rich chocolate cupcakes.)

450 g (1 lb) cream cheese, softened
85 g (3 oz) unsalted butter, softened
1 teaspoon vanilla extract

225 g (8 oz) white chocolate (such as Lindt – do not use a baking chocolate), melted and cooled to lukewarm temperature (see Note)

Note: To melt the chocolate, place it in a double boiler over simmering water on a low heat for about 5–10 minutes. Or use a heatproof bowl set over a saucepan of simmering water (but do not allow the base of the bowl to touch the water). Stir occasionally until completely smooth and no pieces of chocolate remain. Remove from the heat and let cool for 5–10 minutes until lukewarm.

In a large bowl, using the medium speed of an electric mixer, beat together the cream cheese and butter for about 3 minutes until smooth. Add the vanilla and beat well. Add the melted chocolate and beat well. Use immediately or store, covered, at room temperature for up to 4 hours.

MAKES ENOUGH FOR ONE 2-LAYER 23-CM (9-IN) CAKE

Metric Equivalents

LIQUID AND DRY MEASURE EQUIVALENTS

METRIC	US CUSTOMARY
1.25 millilitres	¼ teaspoon
2.5 millilitres	½ teaspoon
5 millilitres	1 teaspoon
15 millilitres	1 tablespoon
30 millilitres	1 fluid ounce
60 millilitres	¼ cup
80 millilitres	⅓ cup
120 millilitres	½ cup
240 millilitres	1 cup (8 fluid ounces)
480 millilitres	1 pint (2 cups, 16 fl ounces)
960 millilitres (.96 litre)	1 quart (4 cups, 32 ounces)
3.84 litres	1 gallon (4 quarts)
28 grams	1 ounce (by weight)
114 grams	¼ pound (4 ounces)
454 grams	1 pound (16 ounces)
1 kilogram (1000 grams)	2.2 pounds

OVEN TEMPERATURE EQUIVALENTS

DESCRIPTION	°CELSIUS	FAN OVEN °C	GAS MARK	°FAHRENHEIT
Very cool	110	90	¼	225
Very cool	120	100	½	250
Cool or slow	140	120	1	275
Cool or slow	150	130	2	300
Warm	160	140	3	325
Moderate	180	160	4	350
Medium hot	190	170	5	375
Fairly hot	200	180	6	400
Hot	220	200	7	425
Very hot	230	210	8	450
Very hot	240	220	9	475

Index

About the Author

Allysa Torey opened the Magnolia Bakery in New York City's Greenwich Village in the summer of 1996. Allysa, when she wasn't baking, could formerly be found around town singing with her fifties jazz band, The Allysa Torey Swing Band. Coauthor of *The Magnolia Bakery Cookbook*, she currently lives in upstate New York with her boyfriend, Tadhg, where she spends her time writing, cooking, gardening and taking long walks through the cornfields with her collie Sam.